the best of
TALL
TALES

Michael Burns is a university teacher, writing coach, actor, editor and storyteller. He has a BA degree from Georgetown University and a MS from University of Massachusetts Amherst in the US. He also holds a PhD in documentary film history from the University of Birmingham in the UK. He has directed five films for international television and his work has been seen in over twenty countries. He is the founder, director and curator of Tall Tales, India's longest-running, true storytelling event series that features live performances and writing workshops of all kinds. Originally from the US, he has made India his second home since 2011.

Find more online at www.michaelpburns.com

the best of TALL TALES

TRUE STORIES FROM INDIA'S LONGEST-RUNNING STORYTELLING SERIES

EDITED BY **MICHAEL BURNS**

RUPA

Published by
Rupa Publications India Pvt. Ltd 2018
7/16, Ansari Road, Daryaganj
New Delhi 110002

Sales centres:

Allahabad Bengaluru Chennai
Hyderabad Jaipur Kathmandu
Kolkata Mumbai

ISBN: 978-93-5304-148-9

First impression 2018

10 9 8 7 6 5 4 3 2 1

The moral right of the authors have been asserted.

Printed at Thomson Press India Ltd., Faridabad

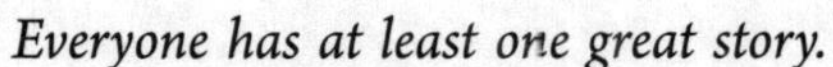

Everyone has at least one great story.

Contents

Introduction

'Everyone has at least one great story.' This tagline has grown from an off-hand slogan that we use at Tall Tales to start our live shows in India, to a kind of mantra that everyone who works with the organization holds dear. Why is that? Because it's true! All of us were born to be storytellers—even though we may not realize it. We see our job at Tall Tales as getting everyone we meet to see just how true this is. Our special talent as a species is telling stories, and because of that, we fundamentally believe that stories are intimately tied up with both our individual and collective destinies.

Tall Tales started as a plan for one night of live storytelling in Mumbai in mid-2013. The idea was to conduct a call for entries where everyday people from the public would submit true, personal, first-person stories, which would be between ten- and fifteen-minutes long. As the curator, I would meet with each shortlisted storyteller to edit and improve what they had put together, and a few weeks later, we'd perform the stories in front of an audience. One Sunday night in Bandra, we did just that—and had a fantastic time. But then something else happened that we didn't expect: More stories started coming in. And coming in. And coming in.

Since that night in June a few years ago, and as of this writing, we've received over 2,200 story submissions, have featured over 240 live stories and have introduced over ninety storytellers to Mumbai. From a kind of glorified open mic, Tall Tales has now grown into the longest-running, live, true storytelling event series in the entire country. Our process has evolved, too. Instead of ten stories (which made for an incredible but *long*, first show), we now feature five stories at every ninety-minute show, repeating the stories one more time in what we call an encore show. These five are selected from among the ten to fifteen submissions we receive every month. The coaching has also been streamlined. We now work extensively with each storyteller (some, of course, more than others) and only bring stories to the stage if we feel they're as strong as they can possibly be. This formula has worked for us, and there's only one way that we know that: Because our stories are superb.

One question that I often get from reporters who are writing about Tall Tales is, 'Which stories do you like the best—the funny ones or the dramatic ones?' I know what they mean and their hearts are in the right place, but the question doesn't actually apply. The best Tall Tales stories can't be labelled as funny or dramatic, because they're *both*—and more. Our best stories have you laughing one minute and crying the next. They leave you shocked and, at the same time, they leave you inspired. They don't push just one button—they push *all* your buttons. And that's the case with the non-fiction short stories you'll read in the following pages.

This book is a collection of twenty of our very best Tall Tales stories. Our contributors span a wide range of backgrounds including students, doctors, designers, therapists, programmers, writers, activists, homemakers and others. Whether it's Maxwel Chhetry on being an extra in Bollywood, Gayatri Aptekar on the power of fortune tellers, Matt Daniels on the perfection of public transportation or Chandrima Das on the terror of stalking, our stories represent deep slices cut out of the lives of our storytellers. What do these stories, the cream of the Tall Tales crop, have in common? They're born from profound honesty, which is probably the most important ingredient in a great story. Comedic stories, scary stories, romantic stories, social justice stories—they all move from interesting to unforgettable when the storyteller is willing to bare his soul; when he's willing to share his innermost desires, fears, hopes and inadequacies, with an audience of complete strangers.

We believe that *all* of our stories have something important to say, but the ones selected for this collection are especially hilarious, insightful, profound and haunting. The selection process was incredibly difficult, to say the least, for one major reason: Our stories are designed to be told out loud. This makes it very difficult to collate a written anthology because some stories may have never been written down at all, existing only in the mind of the storytellers or as a small outline they might have brought to our stage. Equally important is the old adage of communication that's completely apt here, too: 'It's not *what* you say that's important, but *how* you say it.' Like other live storytelling events, our shows are not readings. Rather, our storytellers deliver their stories with the body language, emphasis, pauses and spontaneous asides that make live storytelling so electric. Capturing that on paper is like trying to describe what chocolate tastes like. Is it impossible? No. But the experience is a whole different thing.

Despite the challenge, it's been an exhilarating ride to create this book. Not only does it help us to appreciate just how many stories, themes and genres we've covered over the last four-plus years, but it's also been a fantastic excuse to revisit classic stories and the memories attached to them. Our live events are snapshots in time, much like story sandcastles that are here one second and gone, moments later. Putting our stories in book form not only gives them a longer lifespan but allows the snapshots that we share with just a hundred or so members of our audience, to now be shared with countless readers, including you, who might not have otherwise come across what we do.

Perhaps above all, this book serves as a reminder that what I said at the opening is true. Everyone *does* have at least one great story. Many of our storytellers sat in our audience at one point and silently shuddered when I started the show with our tagline, as they asked themselves in panic—'Oh God! What's *my* story?' For several of them, just a few months later, they were stars on our stage. To watch that happen first-hand is both thrilling and a privilege. And, of course, the best thing about this transformation is that this can happen to any of us. Maybe you're a writer already and so you know what finding your story feels like. Or maybe you're not a writer but you're curious about what it's like to stand in another person's shoes. If this is you, then you're already halfway to your own discoveries. It all starts with a willingness to observe the world closely, to see the things around you with fresh eyes and raw emotions; in other words, to become a storyteller-in-training. That means being vulnerable and being brave, and if you can do that, then you're always—*always*—on the cusp of discovery.

So enjoy this anthology and remember, our stories are the highlight reels of our lives. Take the time to discover yours, and when you do, share them with the world.

— Michael Burns, PhD,
Director, Tall Tales

P.S.: You never know when a lightning flash of inspiration will strike! So, at the end of this book, I've included a few blank pages for you to use right away to capture your story ideas if the need arises.

Bypass

Rohit Nair

Not long back, there was a period when the employment situation in the country was so bad that the prospect of slavery in exchange for two free cups of coffee seemed like a distinct possibility. It was a time when pink toilet paper reminded me of a possible pink slip; a time when I wanted to sleep with a crucifix under my pillow to ward off all nightmares of HR managers. Things were so strange that it was the only time when society would not harshly judge someone for not having a job—because society didn't have one either. It was 2008 and the recession had even become an excuse for constipation.

We had just graduated from college, I and my close friend Pradeep Chandra. We couldn't make the cut when it came to placements as we believed that placements gave room for complacency to creep in and made one overlook the immense gift of being 'synergistic with dissatisfaction'.

Well, actually, to be honest, we were terrible—at a variety of things. But that didn't hinder us from trying. So right after the completion of our exams, we created new resumes, which were adapted from online templates. On our resumes, Pradeep and I had just about the same qualifications, hobbies, and once, even the same mother.

I remember, ten years ago, standing in a queue with Pradeep and our parents to get an engineering seat. I remember my father saying, 'Ek Chemical Engineering, please!' to the lady at the admission desk. It seemed as if he wanted to buy a kilo of onions from an Apna Bazar counter. Onions are way more expensive than engineering seats these days.

And I also vividly remember watching the lady at the desk look at him with utter disbelief. Finally, after blinking those contemplative eyes, she said, 'He has good marks. Take Computer Engineering.'

It was enough to make my Dad go, 'Okay. One Computer Engineering, please.' That was it—five words (none of them being mine) and my future was decided.

Pretty much the same process happened with Pradeep. We had a middle class background. Pradeep's father had a very tedious mechanical job whereas my father had retired from working as a Systems Operations Specialist. Born in the middle class, we were all set to achieve the goals that had been pointed out to us all our lives: 1) Find a job; 2) Find a better job; 3) Update our Bharat Matrimony profiles; 4) Get married to a God-fearing girl who is at least five feet and six inches in height; and 5) Go to the US and finally decide our children's future.

We were not even close to the first milestone.

Like every other citizen of Navi Mumbai, we surged ahead with lots of hope and heavy breakfasts every morning, commuting in the local train among the usual suspects—protracting perverts with sleazy looks on their faces and 9-to-5 lifers whose expressions spoke of total defeat. However, we would not be thwarted by these omens.

We approached companies that ranged right from multistoried edifices to those with shutters and common toilets. There were times when we approached a company and were shooed away by gatekeepers, giving us a whiff of the life of a door-to-door salesman selling non-stick frying pans. During this period, we became adept at identifying IT companies because they had common last names—'metric', 'soft', or 'tech'. We saw Unimetric, Unitech, Sulasoft, Peoplesoft, Ultrasoft, Reallysoft—after a while, they all merged into a big blur.

Cracking the aptitude tests was like finding a window seat in a Virar local—it just wasn't happening. There were times when we would blindly push the glass door and just ask the receptionist what the name of the company was. Pradeep once confessed that the number of rejections he faced had overwhelmingly surpassed the number girls he gawked at. Now *that* was a seriously new low.

With an increasing numbers of refusals, expiring train ticket passes, escalating girlfriend woes and running out of places to compare prices and tastes of samosa pav, we sat absorbed in our blue funk. To make matters worse, Pradeep's father gave up his job due to unforeseen circumstances while my father decided to have a massive heart attack. I had taken a break from wandering in the wilderness to be there in the cardiac ward, where he was recommended for bypass surgery. Meanwhile, Pradeep was still on the lookout. He would call me and give me reasons as to why this time (just like every other time) he failed the aptitude exams. It was tough for both of us, looking after our dads; because, in a way, we had to transcend—or, at least, temporarily take the places of—the men who had been our heroes our whole lives.

Days went by. Pradeep was setting a new record for the number of rejections. I was strangely enjoying the hospital food. Just then we got a call from a company named Geometric Solutions. They had job openings for whiners, depressives and the hapless—in other words, fresh graduates. I didn't want to miss out on this opportunity but my Dad's bypass surgery was scheduled on the same day that we needed to be there. My eldest sister asked me to give the test a good shot as she assured me that she would be around at the time of the operation.

I didn't want to go. But this was Geometric Solutions. They even had 'metric' right in their name.

Pradeep and I finally saw each other again. We could see the agony of this lingering tyranny on each other's faces. I could clearly read, 'My father retired' on his forehead, whereas he read, 'Asian Heart Institute has the best cafeteria' written on my bloated cheeks.

We entered the lobby, trying our best to look like future stiff-necked, shaven mavens who Malcolm Gladwell had talked about. Surrounded by glass doors, fire extinguishers every two metres, spotless floors reflecting another world within them, and with a receptionist wearing a fake smile and lots of foundation, we were already awestruck.

'Wow, look at that foundation,' Pradeep said. It *was* substantial.

We were then taken to one of their training rooms and the distribution of the aptitude test papers was about to start. We both knew how big this was for the two of us. It was our only chance to counter those stereotypes that said, 'Campus placement rejects are only prospective BPO employees'. The room was filled with forty-five other people who looked just like us—the same mixture of semi-competence and desperation. We were an army of the over-educated.

The paper distribution had just started. Pradeep looked at me. I looked back at him. I could see sparks in his eyes and knew what was coming. Pradeep, with his eyes glued to mine, said, 'Dude, I bet the samosa pav out here is really expensive.'

I suspected he was right.

We got our papers and within the stipulated sixty minutes, we completed our tests. It was challenging, but within the range of what we had expected. We had to wait for about twenty minutes at the reception before being called by one of their senior employees. We gathered into the same room where our tests were conducted. They started calling out names—'Vishal Sahani, Ravindra Shanbag...' Both of us were now hoping to hear our names as well. 'Jagannath Nadar, Nilesh Tawade...' Pradeep was getting restless and his nervousness was evident when he whispered, 'Please. Just say our names.'

Just then I heard, 'Shekhar Shinde and Rohit Nair.'

I jolted on my seat and slapped my chest as my internal celebrations started. This was my Rocky Balboa moment. Just then I spotted a girl showing her displeasure at my celebration. I stopped immediately. I'm sure she was thinking, 'Look at him... sheesh... I bet he's from Navi Mumbai.'

I waited while they finished the list. Pradeep held his breath. I held my breath. Pradeep's name wasn't called out. With a half-smile on his face, he patted my back and congratulated me. The coordinator asked the nominees to follow him.

As we moved out of that room, I noticed, on each door,

a name plate with a designation. I looked towards the left—General Manager; towards the right—HR Manager; left again—Head of Operations; and finally, right—Ladies, left—Gents. These names shone under a luminescent yellow light. They were uniform in their appearance. As we moved forward, my aspirations were marching towards having my own door with a name plate shining under my own light. But, just then, I saw another door with the text in a bold, green-coloured font, saying, 'Exit'.

Before I could turn back or look at the coordinator in disbelief, he nonchalantly said, 'Thank you for coming. Have a nice day.'

Pradeep had qualified for the next round.

The sun was bright outside. And I was suddenly overdressed. I couldn't fathom this unjust treatment towards us challenged mortals. What really struck me was not this failure, but the fact that I would now be all alone in these job searches, devoid of my best friend's company. Before I had time to take this all in, sit back, think some more, sulk, cry, squeal, thump my chest and tell my fellow rejects to have some self-respect and to stop laughing, I got a call from my sister and she broke the news of my father's surgery being a success. The doctors had borrowed a vein from his hand and bypassed the defaulting blood vessel by creating a new route. My feeling sorry for myself would have to wait. After all, my Dad being okay, put things in perspective.

More importantly, Pradeep got kicked out in the next round anyway—so I was very happy.

∿

Rohit Nair is a system architect living in Bengaluru.

The Age of Aquarius

Gayatri Aptekar

Eleven days after I was born, my Amma went to an astrologer—again.

A lot of families in India have a family astrologer. It's a very popular tradition to make a visit after a child is born. My mother had actually gone to see him while she was pregnant and he proudly announced that I would be a boy. My chromosomes said otherwise. When I was born, she took me inside to see him.

She then… washed her hands of me.

I'm probably very lucky that I don't live in certain parts of India where much worse can happen; for me, the parties involved, 'compromised', and allowed me to live. But, nowhere near my mother. My grandparents took me in and no one told me anything else.

For the next five years, I grew up in Thanjavur, Tamil Nadu, in Southern India. This is a place well known for its temples and the classical dancing form called Bharatanatyam. Some of my very first memories are of sitting on the cool stone floor of the temple, watching recitals, where the dancers expressed their feelings through abhinaya. It fascinated me. I never sensed the absence of parents or a sibling (though I had one sister). My days were busy playing with my friends and during bedtime, Grandma told me stories of kings and demons. I loved this little world of mine. Occasionally, I asked Grandma about my Amma and Appa. She was smart enough to change the topic and continue the stories.

The answers to my questions came two months before my fifth birthday, when my grandparents announced that we were going to Mumbai to see my parents. I remember that I didn't want to go, but as a soon-to-be five-year-old, I didn't have a choice.

Growing up in a village, Mumbai seemed like a fairy tale. The massive buildings, the constant sounds, the pulsing signs and the incredible traffic were all new to me. People here were running a race—everyone trying to catch the train or a bus or pushing one another in order to be first to stand in an endless line. And then, there in that crowd at Kalyan station, I saw him, my Appa. My Grandpa pointed him out. That was the first time I had ever seen him. I was too shy to really look at him so I hid behind my Grandma.

Appa came closer to me, took me in his sturdy arms and kissed my cheeks. This was the first time someone held me so close.

My eyes kept searching for someone else. I guess Appa sensed it.

'Amma is at home, waiting for you,' he said. We got into the rickshaw and went to their house.

Like Appa said, Amma *was* at home. But she wasn't waiting for me.

'Why did you bring her here?' were the first words I heard my mother say. She threw a pillow on the floor and sat on it, looking out the window. I was with the people who gave birth to me, but I felt like a stranger in their lives—because I was.

My birthday was an afterthought, and Amma's indifference kept increasing every day. She never spoke to me. I looked to her, to hear my name from her mouth, but she made herself too occupied to even notice my presence. I tried to strike up a conversation with my elder sister Vidya, but she was nine years older than me, and a stranger too. I was a baby to her and she was busy with her studies and her friends.

After staying with me for a few days, my grandparents left for Thanjavur.

I tried to sleep, but couldn't get comfortable. I missed the stories, the temple music, the dance and my own friends—my world was small but it was mine. Now I was somewhere else. I remember rice and sambhar with appalam put in front of me to eat, but not feeling hungry. Maybe I was acting out for the attention—God knows that I wanted it. As time went by, I got thinner and sicker and weaker.

Two months later, Amma was diagnosed with a very rare blood disease. I remember watching her holding her chest and struggling to breathe, as if someone had stuffed a cloth in her mouth. The medical facilities in India in those days were not so advanced and the doctors couldn't figure out what to do.

One Sunday morning before my tenth birthday, during my summer vacations, Amma had a stroke and her body started turning blue. Appa left to call the doctor while I stayed with her. One moment, I could feel her heartbeat, and the next, it all went still. She lay there on the mat, with her head on my lap. I could barely move. I had frozen. The heaviness of her head made my left leg numb.

By the time Appa reached with the doctor, it was all over. I held Appa tightly and his eyes welled up with tears. He asked me to stay with the doctor and went to the telephone to call my uncle and grandmother and sister.

As soon as Grandma entered the house, she started crying and shouting, and beating her chest with both her hands. She turned to me and said, 'Are you happy now? You killed my daughter!' Appa stood in the corner of the room. He was too shattered to even react, I guess. I was confused.

The ladies in the house gave Amma's dead body a bath and then draped her in a new saree. They then put a big kumkum teeka on her forehead. The pandit came by 3.00 p.m. and all the formalities were done by early evening.

I ran to Appa when he came home from the funeral. He was quiet. I asked him why Grandma said that I had killed Amma. His reply shook me completely.

He told me that nine years ago, our family astrologer had warned him and Amma to keep me away from the family. His exact words to my mother were, 'This child has come into the world to kill you. Her stars are unlucky.'

Amma's death changed Appa. He spoke less and spent most of his time buried in a newspaper or a book. His previous tolerance for me was all the more magnified by my mother's indifference, but now that that she was gone, he started to play her part as well. Incredibly, against all logic, my father had now started to believe the prophecy that my mother held onto all those years. Maybe he needed someone to blame for her death. When we can't understand something, sometimes we automatically want to point the finger at someone. The little connection I had had with my father started to dissolve as he drifted away.

School still continued to be my sanctuary and I dreaded to come back to an empty house where my Amma's memories had now taken over. I started to daydream visions of her, constructing memories that we never had together, wondering how she could have been manipulated into doing what she did, imagining how a fraud astrologer could live with himself after tearing apart a family in exchange for a few hundred rupees. I was a bubbling soup of emotions and I would cry at the drop of a hat, yell for minor reasons and throw tantrums out of nowhere.

Eventually, studies didn't interest me nor did conversations with anyone—except one person. My sister became my confidante at this point. She urged me to tell her what was bothering me. Not that she had answers to my questions, but having someone to talk to, helped—a lot. Every evening, once my sister returned from college, we spoke for hours as she got busy preparing dinner. She was there to listen, and slowly this became my routine and I loved it.

A few years later, Appa started searching for a groom for Vidya. When he found a suitable match, he broke the news of my sister's wedding one day. The mere thought that she would go away from me brought back familiar sensations in the pit of my stomach. It was as if my heart was about to explode, but I managed to smile and congratulate my sister. The next few days, I hardly spoke to anyone. My appetite was gone and I felt like I was walking around in a daze. I wanted to talk about it to my sister, but everything was eclipsed by plans about shopping, sarees and malls in Dubai. Yes, that was the worst part for me: That she would be about 2,000 kilometres away.

As I helped with all the wedding preparations, my tantrums and mood swings increased. Conversations seemed empty and pointless. There were a million thoughts running through my mind, but I couldn't share anything with anyone. I started bunking college and spent hours travelling from my home to Marine Drive. I spent huge chunks of my day sitting there, staring at the waves that hit the rocks incessantly.

The only person who was there to listen to me finally went far away. I remember asking Appa to loan me some money to call Vidya, but he refused. So I stole it. I didn't care how much I had to take—I needed to connect with her. She was busy with her new life and told me how beautiful and wonderful Dubai was.

I was paralysed and empty. I wanted to end this feeling of helplessness and the easiest way to do that was to end my life. The next morning I took a blade and cut my wrist. As I watched the blood ooze out, the pain slowly subsided. It was a liberating feeling, but sadly I survived. A few months later, I tied a dupatta to the living room fan and tried to put an end to my life again. However, after two unsuccessful attempts at suicide, I had no other option but to live.

Every day I struggled to eat, sleep and even do normal tasks like brushing my teeth or combing my hair. In India, all problems have only one solution—marriage. I wasn't ready to be married, but the forces of our society pushed me unstoppably towards it, and despite all that I was going through, I did somehow manage to fall in love with an incredible person.

People are complicated. Part of you can be content, while another part is raging out of control. But we can only keep them separated temporarily.

We talk so much about giving love, but we seldom speak about receiving love. After all these years I was finally getting love, but I didn't know how to reciprocate. I struggled to express my love to my husband. The suicidal thoughts stuck to me like iron to a magnet. I thought it was just a passing cloud, but it was a giant monster that was eating me up inch by inch every single day. It didn't help that when I was married, my father told my husband about my mother's death and that my stars were unlucky.

My mind kept thinking of ways to end this throbbing pain.

I actually signed myself up for various adventure activities such as rappelling, valley crossing, ropes courses and difficult treks, knowing fully well that sometimes there are accidents on these trips. (I was actually trying to put myself in close proximity to disaster.) I remember climbing to Echo Point in Matheran, Maharashtra, on 7 May 2006 and thinking how easily I could die if I just, ever so slightly, slipped from the top of the hill.

I wondered if it would be painless.

Two months later, I found out I was pregnant. My friends said things would settle down when the child came. But the birth of my daughter didn't change anything fundamental for me—in fact it added to my misery. I was helpless. I couldn't manage myself and here was a life totally dependent on me for everything.

I started behaving hysterically. I remember one incident when I flung a chair towards my husband and it broke. I struggled fighting this alone. I didn't enjoy the little milestones of my daughter's young life. The mantra of ending my life was a parasite sucking out the joy around me. Some days I imagined running up the stairs to my terrace and jumping off—would I fly? Some days I thought of just letting go of the hand support as I stood on the footboard of the speeding Mumbai local train.

On one of my worst days, I went to the newly opened Crossword bookstore in Mulund. I remember that there were beautiful diaries made of handmade paper. The moment I held a diary in my hand, I felt the urge to write, to pour out all that was bothering me.

I immediately picked it up and sat down. At first I struggled to write, but as days progressed, the dam broke and words kept flowing. Writing became therapy to me and by articulating my pain, my emotions slowly came under control. My daughter's unconditional love kept refueling my hope. No matter how much I yelled at her, she would still come and melt away in my arms. After three years of maintaining a journal, I started my blog and discovered that there are many other people out there who have dealt with similar symptoms and are leading perfectly normal lives now.

Gradually I picked up the broken pieces and with the thread of my words, weaved my life together again and gained control over myself—as much control as any of us have. Most importantly, I learned what it really means to forgive and to let go. I learned how to transform my thoughts and interpretations of what had happened to me, and it was like someone took my black-and-white life and threw a thousand cans of paint on it. When I got rid of the interpretations that other people had placed on me, my life became my own, and it was more glorious than anything I had ever seen before. I even took a dance class. The memories of Thanjavur were no longer eerie and lonely.

Every day, people read horoscopes in the newspaper. I know some of us do it for fun, but it's incredible to me that some people really do believe in something like astrology to the extent that they would hand over their sense of right and wrong. I think it says something about how difficult life can be for some people that they would rather blame their problems on the gravity of the planets than to take responsibility for the hearts they break. In my opinion, knowing yourself takes a lot of real work, while knowing midheaven, constellations and the fortune cookie wisdom of the Zodiac takes very little work. Maybe it all comes down to that for most people—easy answers offer the path of least resistance. As for me, I got lucky, and found a way to navigate around the stars, back towards the Earth, where I live.

Gayatri Aptekar is a parenting coach and child therapist and lives in Mumbai.

Tower of Power

Nasir Engineer

I remember the first time I ran five kilometres. I wasn't in good shape. And I certainly wasn't physically ready to do that kind of a run. I remember that I took jibes at myself when I told friends about it, saying that I was on the verge of having to be carried home on a stretcher. I was only half-joking.

The first time I ran 21K was three years later, in December 2012 in Goa. This time I was ready. I put in a solid amount of effort for the training and I was happy with my time. The run was certainly an eye-popping revelation because from that day on, my unshakeable relationship with running began. With this run, I believed I was getting better at building my physical strength and stamina and I could feel a new 'me' coming out of it—as cheesy as that might sound.

Then came a 42K run in Bengaluru, my first ever at that distance—and it came exactly two years after that first 21K race.

I was really surprised at myself and what I was capable of.

My time was three hours and fifty-nine minutes. Running my first forty-two kilometres under four hours was a monumental achievement for me. I kept thinking that it was a nearly 5K loop that had to be run eight times over—which, I think, made it sound even worse in my mind—but I did it.

Since I moved to Bengaluru, I have stayed consistent with my running schedule, getting in at least three runs a week in the early mornings.

In January 2015, I was running at Ulsoor Lake, a prominent landmark in Bengaluru, and I met a guy named John Worsham. He's from the US and had been living in India for over four years. He mentioned that the next day he and some friends were going on a hike to a spot a few hours away, called Kolar, and asked if I wanted to come along. The minute he said the magic word—hike—I said I would absolutely come along.

The next morning was 25 January and there were five of us who set out from the meeting point at Hutchins Road towards Kolar at 8.00 a.m. by car. About seventy-five kilometres away, we reached an area on the highway from where we could see a cluster of hills covered by boulders and tall grass. From a distance, I thought these hills looked like they were a twenty- or thirty-minute climb, but when I reached the bottom of one of the hills, I was so wrong. The grass was much taller and thicker up close, and the rocks were larger than they looked from the highway. At 9.00 a.m., we set off.

We finished climbing two of the hills' peaks at around 2.30 p.m. and then we left for home. We were all starving, especially me. During the walk, I had eaten an apple, half a packet of Britannia cake and this very American thing called mountain trail mix; I was still hungry.

But I wasn't the only one, so thankfully someone from our group had heard of a place called Plan B at Indiranagar. I'm not a foodie, to be honest, but I like to eat. (There's quite a difference between the two, the way I see it.) It was just about 5.00 p.m. when we made it to Plan B. Right outside, before entering, we noticed a signboard with the name of the restaurant and underneath, in brackets, it said, 'Home of the Mother Clucker'. We all cracked up a little while heading inside. The place looked really cool with a lot of funny quotes hanging on the walls, a bar counter, large wooden tables with bench seats, and the whole place dimly lit with a list of vintage American tracks playing on the jukebox. Think TGI Fridays, but without the 'glamour'.

All five of us took our places at the table where we could sprawl out. I picked up the menu which was made in the form of a giant antique, wooden-framed poster. Maybe it was the subliminal message from before, but what caught my eye was the name of an intriguing dish, 'Big Bad Mother Clucker'. I pointed it out and we laughed again. I then went on to read the description: '700 grams of chicken, cheese, egg and fries'. I'd seen things like that on TV but never in person. This is definitely not the India of our grandparents.

The waiter came over and we ordered. When it was my turn, I told him I was going for the BBMC. He just shook his head the way you would if you had just read a tragic story in the newspaper. He said I wouldn't be able to finish it, but wrote it down on his pad anyway.

Within a few minutes, our beers arrived. I had ordered a Budweiser. I am not normally a beer drinker but, to be honest,

I was savouring every sip. I figured if I was going with American food, I should just go the whole hog (no pun intended), and get a drink to match it. I'm sure there are better beers out there, but the Bud tasted just right.

When I finished my drink, the smell of food hit my nose, and as the fragrance grew stronger, I got all the more excited that it was going to be my order that was coming from behind. As the waiter leaned forward, placing the wooden plank that had my burger on it right in front of me, he announced, 'Here's your Big Bad Mother Clucker, Sir.'

One look at that burger and all five of us were speechless. Just as an aside for a minute—have you ever been to the Rambo Circus that makes its way around India every year? Well, the final act of the circus is... well, it's not really an *act*. It's more of a spectacle. A guy drinks a huge amount of liquid—I mean *huge*—maybe five litres or more, including several live goldfish, and then projectile vomits them up into various containers. It's pretty disturbing and when it's over, he expects the audience to erupt in applause at this accomplishment. And they *do* clap, but it's not so much an appreciation, but kind of a combination of disgust, confusion and relief that the act is over. It was a similar kind of mix of emotions that we experienced when we all saw the burger. We were dumbfounded, impressed, but also a little terrified.

This burger was mammoth. It was so enormous that we spent the first few minutes just taking photos of it. The bottom layer was a burger bun coated with cheese, a few veggies on top of it, followed by a three-quarters-of-an-inch-thick chicken patty, and then four more patties of the same size on top of that. This was followed by a layer of egg, some more veggies, more cheese, and finally, the top burger bun. Besides this, on the massive plate, was a huge pile of fries surrounding everything. This was my meal.

There was no way that the burger was going to fit into my mouth all together. So I slid off the topmost chicken patty that had the egg on it and began eating it. As I was eating, John told me that he had heard about a challenge that the restaurant had, wherein if one could finish this particular burger in six minutes or less, they would win a prize.

He was vaguely sure about it, and then the waiter dropped by and confirmed it. He said that there was a special contest involving this burger and another one, called 'The Animal' (a huge beef burger with a massive bucket of chicken wings). If you take the challenge and finish either of these in six minutes or less, you get a t-shirt, your meal would be free, *and* the staff would take your picture, which would then hang proudly in the restaurant's Hall of Fame. The downside was that if you don't finish your food, your photo would hang in infamy in the restaurant's Hall of Shame.

I was in no way up for the six-minute challenge because by the time I found out about it, it was already past ten minutes. Not that I would have done it anyway. It's bonkers enough to cram that much food into your system, but if you had to eat it in five or six minutes, you won't even have the time to taste it. Even within the bizarre logic of eating contests, you have to preserve *some* form of dignity.

I was now into my second patty and I was going strong. My confidence was soaring and with a nonchalant look, I chomped it all down. When I finished the third out of the five patties, I started to feel really full. But I wasn't going to let that stop me. This was exactly how I made it through my first ultra-marathon. That was seventy-five kilometres, the most I had ever run. To run those kind of distances, you need a strategy. So I tried to apply that logic to this burger.

In order to tackle this burger mentally, I placed the top bun aside for a moment and picking up the two patties that were left, took some colossal bites. Each mouthful was getting tougher to chew and gulp. My jaw was pretty numb and I tried not to think about how, with every bite, the cholesterol and fat were very likely clogging my arteries and making my organs react in an emergency, pre-diabetic way. I thought about the Mumbai Marathon that I had run just six days before. On the run, I was cruising for the first thirty kilometres and then suddenly, before I realized what was happening, I hit a wall. I slowed down drastically, and went from thirty-one to thirty-five kilometres. I was in a torturous state of mind. My legs weren't responding. I did not want to run anymore. I didn't care about my time or anything else. I seriously thought about stopping, just pulling up at the side and calling it a day. But right before I decided to give up, at about the thirty-six-kilometre mark, all of a sudden I found a second wind, a sudden surge of energy right when I thought I had run out of it. With every step, I could feel my energy getting stronger, coming from some hidden inner-reserve that I didn't know was there.

The idea of putting the last two half-eaten patties within the buns did not work in my favour, so I put aside the top bun and began eating the second-to-last patty by itself. I could feel my body disobeying my command to take the burger in. Each bite was getting more impossible to gulp.

Now, in a run, there are people—friends or relatives of the runners, of course, but sometimes complete strangers, too—who come to cheer and encourage every athlete going by. I love these cheers. One loud cry of 'You can do it!' seems like nothing from the outside, but when you're running, it can help you push harder for the next couple of kilometres or more.

I had my own set of spectators at Plan B. I was so concentrated on my plate that at first I didn't notice that everyone had finished their food and were all just watching me at the table. I asked them if they wanted to leave and I would stop eating right there but they said they'd rather wait and root for me to finish the beast off. That sent a little surge of energy through me and I powered my way through the remaining patties, right towards the home stretch.

I was now down to the last three bites.

My eyes clearly indicated I wasn't going to do this ever again. If it had been a cartoon, my pupils would have been little hamburgers and stars would have been spinning in a circle above my head. I was in a daze, pretty much, when I took the third-to-last bite. That bite took me a full two minutes to get down because my body was refusing to let it in. Then came the second-to-last bite. It wasn't any better. The voices of the people talking around me began to fade out. And I was now down to my last piece. This bite was unusually large. I deliberately left it a little big because I wanted to finish this feat off with a little flair like the way I would finish a marathon. In a run, I always make it a point to sprint the last two hundred metres or so and cross the finish line with a little pizzazz.

I held it in my hand. This was it. As I put that last bite in my mouth, my friends erupted with joy. They hooted and clapped. This was when the waiter came by and he said, 'I've got to hand it to you. Larger men—much larger—haven't been able to finish it and I had to pack up their burgers. But you, seeing the size you are, managed to do it. Nice job.' The only thing I regret from the visit was that we were so excited that we forgot to take my photo to put on the wall at the restaurant. I'll just have to go back, I think—and send them this story as evidence.

I love this quote: 'Running doesn't keep me dependent on anyone, unlike other sports. There's no sports arena I have to go to; no equipment I have to concern myself with. It's all up to me, the way I want to deal with and overcome my challenges, to be stronger.'

Said by me.

I do like challenges. Not the kind where there's an obvious one-upmanship going on, but the challenges where *I* get to be better—and that's a special kind of challenge that doesn't come around very often.

As of today, I have had no desire to eat a burger. Writing this story out actually sends a slight chill down my spine as the image of that burger flashes by like a kind of nightmare. I'm sure I will eat a burger again someday, and if I do, it has to be special. It has to be something worth writing home about.

Something like the Big Bad Mother Clucker.

∽

Nasir Engineer lives in Bengaluru and is an improv comedian and promotes running through social media.

Catdog

Alisha Parekh

There are only two things you have to know about Pranay Parekh. First, he is an incredibly good storyteller. And second, and more importantly, he's my older brother.

Growing up with him was no easy task. If I could put this in the simplest possible way: I am a cat and he is a dog. I like being by myself, doing what I like. I love the couch. I'm moody, stubborn and indifferent (although I secretly need love… and food). He, on the other hand, follows me around, can't leave me alone, wants to constantly touch, kiss, lick, cuddle, has to be on the couch if I am on it, is lively, caring, warm, energetic, and always gives me the attention that I don't want.

There was no end to our fights—unless something in the

house broke or our screams crossed the boundaries of the four walls.

Maybe it wasn't like cat and dog but more like cat and mouse. Our fights were like Tom and Jerry's. We would be running round, pushing, throwing, smashing whatever came in our way. Doors banging, windows rattling; these were a common phenomenon—almost routine. If ironing boards could come out of walls and flatten heads, I'm sure we would have explored that, too. Leaving us home alone was a roll of the dice that my parents dreaded to make.

I still clearly remember one of our fights. I was sitting in the hall when my brother decided to give me a body slam. Oh, and I almost forgot to mention, my brother was heavy—130 kilograms at the time—but that never seemed to stop him. Body slamming was his specialty. He would run to wherever I was and dive on me, as if I was an extension of the sofa or the bed. One day he crushed me like a bug and then picked me up and slammed me down. Maybe it was just irresistible for him to see me so comfortable. I don't know.

And then, out of nowhere he would assault me with kisses and hugs at the drop of a hat. Of course that's even *worse*—to dare to punctuate the abuse with love—and was enough to set me off. I pushed him off me and the chase began: His room, my room, the hall, the dining room, the living room, the balcony. This went on until he took refuge behind his door, while I stood outside kicking it ferociously.

'Open the door, you chicken, hiding behind it like a coward. Why can't you leave me alone? You're *so* dead today!'

'You wish! First come and get me.'

The door would always save him.

Most of our fights were pretty much like that; only the

weapons were upgraded over time. We were carrying out *Mortal Kombat*-sized planned attacks, complete with strategizing, finding weaknesses and strengthening defences. This was the Mountain versus Oberyn Martell times ten.

Over the years, our alliance changed, as it does with most siblings—from foes to friends. We continued fighting with the same intensity, but now we also fought *for* each other. We became each other's best buddies. He was my father, mother, brother, sister, guide, best friend and role model. My universe revolved around him and his universe existed exclusively for me.

His passion for stories could not be curtailed. Those days, he wanted to be a film-maker, and to narrate stories on the big screen. He devoured every movie that came his way.

He made a short film in 2009 called *Kalki*, for a private short film camp that happened in Bengaluru. It earned him an award and a lot of recognition. It also got him a seat at Whistling Woods, a major film-making institute sponsored by Subhash Ghai.

But he had other plans. He joined Mudra Institute of Communications in Ahmedabad, more popular as MICA, and took a course in ad filming, where he said there was more scope for creativity than in 'clichéd' Indian cinema.

In my eyes, he was the George Orwell of modern times. I loved him, but we still fought because it was, in a strange way, our way of showing each other how much we cared. I think only siblings know what I'm talking about.

Just before he left for Ahmedabad in 2009, we had another fight. This one left a mark; rather, a scar.

I was having breakfast with my cousin, who had come down to visit us, and Pranay was in an unusual state of mind: Moody and touchy over the most insignificant of topics. I don't quite remember what our argument began with, but in no time, he was raging with anger.

'You don't value me one bit,' he said, while watching TV. 'Have you ever said, "I love you" to me? Do you even care about my feelings? You're an arrogant brat. Wait till I'm gone. You'll realize my value when you don't have me around anymore.'

'That'll be a peaceful life, you know.' I winked and let out a laugh.

His temper was unnecessary and the conversation was senseless. His gripped tightened over the remote and before he could control his movements, he threw it with full force. It smashed hard against the table and rebounded towards me, hitting me right on my mouth and slitting my lower lip vertically.

Time stopped.

I was bleeding heavily. The remote had hit me hard enough to chip my tooth. I ran towards the bathroom, staining the floor on the way. He ran after me.

'I am so sorry! Are you okay?'

In the background, we heard our mother pick up the phone and say, 'He hit her and she's bleeding. Come home now.'

As I was cleaning up, he caught a glimpse of my face in the mirror. It broke him down to know he had done that to his baby's face. He hugged me and wept.

'I am so sorry. I am so sorry. You are my little baby sister. How could I hurt you?'

I had never seen that side of him in seventeen years of my life—him, in his most vulnerable moment.

In my head, it was all so funny. Everyone out of character; all masks dropped. But I also felt sorry for him. He was in more pain than I was, I think.

He ran into his room and locked himself up.

It took me a while to clean up. Just as I walked out of the

bathroom, my Dad walked in. He looked at me, a half-smile crossed his face as I showed him mine.

'What happened?'

I thought about our endless fights; the war of attrition that had seesawed both ways. 'Nothing much. A basketball hit me.'

'That must have been one big basketball.'

Our alliance had been sealed.

Skip ahead two months after he left. I missed him every day. I dropped him messages through his friends and mine, letting him know I was upset. Finally, when he called, we spoke for hours, discussing his girlfriends, movies and all the amazing perks of starting a new life. He was living his dream and I was proud of him. We fought on that day too, of course. But it was virtual, which was good news for my lip and skull.

Raksha Bandhan was around the corner and this was the first time he wouldn't be with me. I wanted him home and, so, was trying by all means possible to convince him to come. Finally he agreed in exchange for a new laptop. Classic.

On 2 August, in our Bengaluru house, we sat at the dining table discussing his trip home. Mom and I were creating a menu with all his favourite dishes while Dad was on the phone with my grandparents. We were acting like he hadn't come home in years—I guess it felt that way to us.

The landline rang. My Dad answered it.

'Hello… Yes, speaking… Hello, Sir… What? What happened?'

We were still.

'Who is it?' Mom asked, looking at Dad's pale face.

'I'll be there right away.'

Pranay had been admitted to the hospital. He had developed a breathing problem in his sleep. My Mom started to ask a question but it was cut off by another phone call. I could hear the voice on the other end.

'No, Mr Parekh. I insist you come, and soon. Right now.'

'I don't understand. Is he… is he alive?'

My father's question was answered by silence on the other side.

I'll never forget my mother's screams. She was howling like a wounded animal. I spent the rest of that day either making or receiving phone calls. Each conversation felt like a stab in my chest. There are some situations in life where you have no choice but to keep taking the blows over and over again.

The same evening we flew to Mumbai to receive Pranay's body. Pallavi, my aunt, had gotten special permission from the airport authorities to allow him to be flown in a passenger plane's cargo. The thought of him flying in the cargo made us all shudder. Outside the airport, the entire family assembled, awaiting his arrival. We all were scattered in little groups, hugging and mourning over the loss of the first-born in the family. It is hard to put into words what ran through each of our minds that evening, for there is no harsher reality than to see your lineage lie lifeless in a cold coffin.

We took him home to finish the last rituals. Before they sealed the coffin, I tied him the Rakhi I had saved for him. It was, after all, Raksha Bandhan—our last one together. His hands were frozen and hard, like stone.

That night, after we put our relatives to sleep, I, my cousins, and our friends sat around him in a circle. Holding hands, we bid him farewell the way he deserved to have it, by laughing and sharing memories.

His death changed me in ways I can't fully explain but this is my best shot.

For some people, when something like this happens, it's like their enthusiasm for life is sucked out; like a rug pulled out from underneath them and they're left to navigate through the emptiness of whatever's left—half of what they once were. But for me, ironically, I was reborn that day, with more life than I ever had before.

I feel as though his spirit left his body only to find a new home in mine. I'm no longer a cat, but a catdog. A rare but correct combination of energy, passion, strength, awareness and, above all, loyalty. I know that it seems crazy to say this but I love him even more right now than I ever did before. He's everywhere; when before, he was just somewhere. He is around me all the time, communicating to me through signs and dreams. I see him in the world and, most importantly, I see him whenever I need to.

We often hold on to so many things in life: anger, grudges, regrets, aspirations; 'one day' we'll do this or do that. But the truth is that the only moment that we can count on is this one, right now. We are born and we will die; and that is certain. What story we write in between is our own. It is, after all, the journey that matters—not just the destination.

〜

Alisha Parekh is a student who divides her time between Bengaluru and Mumbai.

Master 214

Matt Daniels

The first thing you should know about me is that I'm kind of a big deal. That is to say, wherever I go in Mumbai, all the time, I get preferential treatment.

I'm aware of it; I've wrestled with it; and I've come to terms with it. Every day of the nine years I've lived in India, I have benefited from a deep-seated colour bias. Yes, people are nice to me because of the colour of my skin. And that's not all. I'm also an object of curiosity, confusion and, occasionally, ridicule. The latter, maybe even more than the average white dude because I dress funny.

The second thing you should know about me is that I smile pretty much all the time, to the extent that if I'm not smiling, you know there's some shit about to go down. I make it a habit to smile at everybody I meet—and not a fake smile, because you can tell; a genuine smile (complete with crinkles at my temples), because I am genuinely happy to see you.

Now, I'm not smiling *because* it results in special treatment, but nevertheless, it does. People go out of their way to help me, and Mumbaikars are already exceptionally helpful. They engage me in conversation, they go out of their way to talk to me, and they *remember* me.

So I don't always know why, at any given moment, I'm getting preferential treatment. It could be because of my skin colour, my beaming countenance, spectacular wardrobe, or even my university degree. But in most cases, I can venture a pretty good guess that it's the first one of those reasons.

For instance, once I was taking the #1 bus up from Colaba around midnight and the conductor plunked himself down next to me—which in itself was not so unusual, maybe, because I was in the last window seat before the rear door, the one with the little scrolly thing naming the destination—and he asked me, 'Which country?' He, then, proceeded to give me a tour of the city, naming each neighbourhood we passed through. I've lived in Mumbai for over eleven years and know the area so well I could navigate it blind, but I was happy to take his tour:

'Mohammed Ali Road… Byculla… there's Rani Bagh… the Jhoo…'

'The what?'

'The Jhoo inside Rani Bagh.'

'Okay, the Jhoo.'

'Chinchpokli… Lal Bagh…' And all the way up to Khar. This guy went above and beyond. I was identifiably a foreigner and, in some sense, a guest.

Special treatment. Preferential treatment, if you will. I'm just saying, it's there.

I know, you're thinking: *What is he doing on the godforsaken #1 bus at midnight? Take a taxi like a normal person! Sit in a taxi, pay your ₹100—wait, this is Juhu after all—pay your ₹400 and don't have a conversation with anybody unless it's 'Bhai sahib, left le lijiye, right le lijiye'*. Well, sorry. Excuse me for being ridiculous and ₹382 richer.

And—I'll put in an unpaid plug here—there are many good reasons to take the bus. You're the king of the road, no puny SUV will mess with you; you're sitting way up above the traffic and the diesel fumes; and you can read! You can read a book, you can read street signs. I could go on.

But the *most* special treatment I have ever gotten on the bus was so special that you couldn't even see it.

For a while, every weekday, I used to take the #211 and #214. Even if you're from Mumbai, and *especially* if you live anywhere south of Parel, you probably have no idea where they go. It's okay. Here are the cliff notes:

#211: Bandra Station to Father Agnel Ashram and Petit School

#214: Chuim Village to Mount Mary via Bandra Station

The bus also takes you to unseen places—places invisible to the secular world of cars and rickshaws, which pass through them like ghosts through walls. For many places in Mumbai, the bus is the only evidence that these places exist at all. For instance, nobody says, 'I live in Dandpada', but somebody hand-painted 'Dandpada' on the bus stop so that's what I learned to say when I wanted to get down there. And for that matter, you'll be hard-pressed to find a sign—literally any street sign— declaring Chuim Village to, in fact, *be* Chuim Village, but that's what the scrolly thing on the front of the bus says: 'Chuim Gaon'. And so there it is.

The one thing that you're *guaranteed* to see on the bus is the conductor. When you take the bus regularly, you get to know the conductors on those corresponding lines. Each of them would show up once a week, give or take, in rotation. And if you're like me, when you don't know the names of people you see frequently, you make up nicknames. Of course, to their faces, these guys were all 'sir'. But in my head…

There was a tall, gaunt old man with a powerful stare who I called Skeletor. There was a kid who didn't look a day over eighteen, with bushy hair and eyes that darted around as he punched tickets, so he became Alvin, as in *Alvin and the Chipmunks*. And then there was one who bore an uncanny resemblance to a friend from college, with floppy hair and a perfectly pressed shirt—so at first I called him Dan Luskin. But before long, I understood that this guy was beyond nicknames. And he became, simply, the Master.

Do you ever get that feeling when you encounter someone from whatever walk of life, who does a job with such blinding precision and efficiency, that you know yourself to be in the presence of greatness? Maybe you know someone like that: a barista, an auctioneer, a mochi, or a paanwala? Maybe you've seen that video of the magic chapati roller on YouTube, rolling and then throwing fifty chapatis over his shoulder at about two per second?

Well, that was the Master.

'Bus conductor' is essentially a job for life. It's not so much that the incentives to excel are really bad; there just aren't any. You're not getting promoted, but you're also not getting punished. If a conductor gets way out of line and does something really offensive, you can take the time and effort to register a complaint—my friend Dipesh has done this twice now, but he's one in a million. And while I've found conductors to be, without exception, scrupulously honest, basically they're immune to criticism. They just come in every day and do a decent job.

But not the Master. 'Decent' did not cut it.

The job of a conductor is, first of all, giving out tickets, which they keep in a little case by their side. They pick it up, rummage through the stacks of booklets and tear one off. That was a normal conductor. The Master, before you even *saw* him open his case, he'd already torn out the ticket and slammed the case shut: kaChunk. He'd go through the bus and you'd hear kaChunk, kaChunk, kaChunk; a rapid-fire mowing down of passengers one after the other.

Then, of course, there's taking the money for the tickets. With the Master, there was no bickering, as you often get, about change—'*chhey rupaya chhutta de*'—because the Master not only had the exact change but he knew which pocket he was taking it from, without looking.

A big part of the conductor's job is giving directions, because a huge number of people in this city simply do not know where they're going. It was the Master's habit to remain, for the most part, speechless. He nodded to affirm and cocked his head to the side to say, 'Get down now'. That was the usual extent of his expressions.

But the #214 was far from silent. The kaChunk of the ticket case was just the beginning, the overture. The Master could make three distinct sounds with his punch. There was the standard click, meaning 'Who needs a ticket?'—though it was a rare phenomenon on the Master's bus that anyone was left without a ticket. There was a loud clack against the poles of the bus that meant, 'It's getting crowded in here, so move it up, *chala pude*'. And then there was a totally unique third noise, a metallic boing, like a morchung or what we call a Jew's harp, that he would use to punctuate a transaction, to put an exclamation point on it, while letting the straphangers in the packed aisle know he was making his way through. I don't know how he did that one; I'd never heard it before and have never heard it since.

And the final thing a conductor has to do is, of course, to ring the bell to alert the driver that the passengers boarding at the back have all shoved their way in, or are, at least, hanging securely off the door, and that he can move ahead. The bell is tied to a rope that runs down the length of the bus and there's a thunk-thunk sound you make *before* you ring, by whipping that rope against the roof of the bus to let those folks clambering in know that you don't have all day and they're exhausting your already very frayed patience. The *moment* the last passenger alit, there was a ding-ding, and the Master gave that rope the two most precise, minute yanks; the bell would just barely tinkle, and we'd be on our way.

In summary: click-click, clack, boing, kaChunk, thunk-thunk and ding-ding. The #214, under the Master's control, was a one-man percussion orchestra. It was like a front-row seat at a Sivamani concert—if Sivamani also sold his own tickets.

I appreciated the Master's work and I wanted to find some way to commend him, either in person or—as you can, and as I've done, for bus drivers in New York City—to nominate him for some kind of award. But there's no such award in Mumbai, as far as I could tell, and furthermore, drawing any sort of attention to the Master seemed to be somehow crass, or outside of what I'd imagine to be his code. Even asking his name would have been way out of bounds. But I think he knew how I felt about him by the way I behaved in response.

For somebody who values precision like the Master, responding with precision is itself a form of compliment. When I was on the #214 in the shadow of the Master, I always made sure I was paying attention, that I was completely focused on the transaction at hand, that I had my money extended, that I pronounced my destination, usually the train station, with complete clarity—'su-te-san'—and then I sat back and let the magic happen. And, of course, I smiled. He never smiled back, but what he *did* do, when he approached and turned to me, was nod. He gave me a nod so nearly imperceptible that nobody else could have seen it. But I saw it, and it was unmistakably a nod of recognition. It was special treatment.

After I moved away from Chuim Village, I found the occasional reason to come back, but rarely by bus. And, frankly, I started to avoid Bandra altogether, because how often do I need to pay four times as much for dinner? But certain things about Bandra are irreplaceable. One thing I do every time I'm about to visit the States is to load up on junk for my younger cousins from Hill Road: necklaces, bangles, misspelled t-shirts, dangerous Chinese toys, etc. Hill Road's got it all.

So I was walking down Hill Road one Sunday afternoon in late May—in late May you're wading through ultra-thick air that's settled down, moist and dense like a bebinca, and at the same time you're also slogging through a dense cloud of teenage girls. And it's *work*, just walking. I reached the point that most people visiting India know quite well, where my shirt was soaked through and I'd had enough of the traffic, the heat, the crowds, and I thought: *You know what would be perfect right now? I'll go down to Yacht, the bar at the end of the road, and have a cold beer.* Just thinking about it had the effect of a cool breeze. But it was physically impossible. The crowd was too thick, and with the traffic straining against it, there was no way to push forward. And even if I'd found an empty rickshaw, no self-respecting rickshaw-wallah would be willing to take me half a kilometre in this traffic.

Nothing doing, until out of nowhere a bus came lurching past. So I hopped on. And who should it be, making his way through the aisle to take my ticket, but—the Master. I couldn't help but smile. The hottest day of the year and he's in his perfectly pressed brown uniform—not a spot on it— and not a drop of sweat anywhere on his forehead. He had the same precise mannerisms as always, but he was—or was it just my impression?—a little bowed down by the indignities of the intervening years. His punch—his instrument—had been replaced by a computerized printout machine, which I found ineffably sad—like taking the trumpet away from Dizzy Gillespie.

But I was so excited to repeat our ritual that I wasn't prepared for what happened next. He turned to me and looked me in the eye to ask for my destination, and—there was nothing there. No nod. No glimmer of recognition. Nothing. My smile faded, and for a split second, my voice caught. I hesitated. And with the Master, you never hesitate. After a second, I found the words, 'St. Andrew's Church'. He handed me my ticket and change, and he silently moved on.

Here was a guy whose name I didn't know, who shouldn't have meant anything to me at all. But the recognition I'd received from him, unlike any other, had been truly special. It had less to do with my novelty, or so I'd imagined, and more to do with an understanding, a mutual appreciation.

I don't know; is that ridiculous? Maybe.

So I shuffled up the aisle to the front of the bus, stood there for a minute as Yacht came into view, and moved towards the door to get down while the bus was still rolling—because that's the efficient thing to do if nobody's getting on, right? I mean, don't stop if you don't have to? And as both my feet hit the pavement, the bell tinkled twice and the engine roared into motion. I turned to the road, contemplating the eternal mystery of whether we can ever know another human being.

And as the #214 crawled ahead, I glanced back. And there, standing at the rear door of the bus ... was the Master, with his hand to his forehead in a salute, which I returned.

And then I went and had a beer.

Matt Daniels is a restaurateur, writer, graphic designer and game-maker, who divides his time between Goa and Detroit.

How I Met My Mother

Priya Ramanathan

Growing up, I always swore I'd never be the kind of mother that mine was to me. She was dominating and pushy, not to mention excruciatingly critical. *When I have a baby, I will be cool, democratic and breezy,* I told myself. But the reality turned out to be something else altogether.

After years of obsessing over wanting a baby, my son finally came home to me on 23 December 2010. I had conceived him four and a half years earlier, he was born seven months and eighteen days before that, and I got pregnant with him five months and eight days prior to that. If that sounds convoluted, it's because it is.

So, I have wanted a baby since forever. Even before I got

my first period, I remember my friends would tease me that if I ever took a random pregnancy test, even without the mandated precursory 'workout' regime, I'd still come out positive. They meant it as a joke, but I think it might not be too far from the truth. When all my classmates and friends were harbouring ambitions of becoming VPs and CEOs, my only desire was to be happily married and be a mother of two by the age of thirty. I pictured myself packing home-cooked meals, braiding my daughter's hair, and waving to my children as they left for school.

None of that happened.

At thirty-one, I found myself single after a bitter breakup and viciously hateful of men. It was then that I decided to go with plan B: Ditch marriage and head straight for motherhood.

I decided to adopt.

When I first told my traditional Tamilian parents of my intentions, Appa was intrigued and Amma was horrified. She begged me to wait for a few months so she could find me a suitable Tamil boy. 'Marry him and *then* have babies,' she said. 'That's how it's done.'

Now, I'm usually very rebellious with my mother, but on this occasion, I decided to go with it because I felt it was a fair ask. In the coming days, I watched her move heaven and Earth to find me the ideal life partner. Six months turned to a year, a year turned into two, and two years turned into four. And then, finally after kilos of upma, vada, idli and gallons of filter coffee had been given out to no avail, Amma finally abandoned the manhunt, hung up her boots, and gave me and my adoption plans her blessing.

That's how I got pregnant with my son on 15 July 2010. It was the day that I first visited the agency in Sion. I was unbelievably excited but my bubble burst about three minutes into my appointment. The director told me I was not an ideal parental candidate because I was single and I could not provide a child with a wholesome family atmosphere. Naturally, I was devastated, but decided to plough through all the same, once I realized that she could dissuade me but not fully stop me.

I registered immediately and started the process which included a whole gamut of legal procedures. I had to arrange for court affidavits for guardianship, get referrals and testimonials from friends, and had to organize statements from family and medical health professionals who would certify my competence. I had to also get tested for life-threatening illnesses to ensure I lived long enough to look after a child. It is a long, drawn-out, rather painful process that can easily scare off or dissuade someone from adopting. But I already felt pregnant, so I refused to go home without a baby. I took things one day at a time and kept my eyes firmly on the prize.

Then one day, barely two months after registering, I was told that a baby had been matched with me. I was also told it would be a boy. Knowing that, one of the first things I did was pick out a name. I would listen to the Vishnu Sahasranama every day and the name that spoke to me the most was Atindriyah, which means, 'beyond the comprehension of the sense organs' and that is what my son is to me. In fact, one of the first things I was told about the child was that he has a hernia—a condition I had as a child. Because of the hernia, he was declared surgically needy and had been passed up by two families. Strangely, that defect became our connection. I didn't give birth to him, but I felt he still had a little bit of me in him.

I first met Atin when he was five and a half months old. I was scheduled to take him for the mandated pre-adoption medical examination. After having rejected and sometimes also being rejected by thirty-two men in my unsuccessful journey to matrimony, I prayed that it would be love at first sight with motherhood. What if he was amazing, but there was just no spark—no connection?

But one look at the tiny baby in a pink bonnet and I knew I had found the love of my life. In biological pregnancy terms, that would be the moment that I felt the baby move inside me; suddenly my motherhood wasn't a concept anymore.

One of the things that the agency did was to instruct potential parents to meet their future children so that both could get to know each other. This was designed especially for the children so they could get comfortable with their possible new parents. It was surreal to be allowed a privilege that biological parents are denied: The joy of holding and talking to a baby before actually becoming a parent. I would meet him, talk to him, coo to him and sing to him. It was an excellent bonding period that taught me three things about my son: 1) He had great taste in music; 2) He hated to go to bed; and 3) Bengali songs put him to sleep the fastest. His favourite song was the Rabindra Sangeet song, 'Aanando lokey'. But the music and the magic would last for precisely sixty minutes, after which he'd be taken away and I'd be left broken, bare-handed and barren.

As I waited for the big day, I decided to use the time to do my homework. So I read up on single parenting, repainted my bedroom, baby-proofed the bathroom, shopped for infant bowls, stocked up on diapers, researched pediatricians and interviewed full-time help. I also socialized like never before, and met friends for breakfasts, lunches, high teas and dinners, knowing soon I would be a busy new mom. I stocked up on a year's supply of girl gang madness.

Then one Wednesday afternoon, I got a call saying my papers

had been accepted and that I could take Atin home the following day. None of us slept that night. And the next day, at precisely 12.10 p.m., amidst misty-eyed maids, sadly envious older kids, and nervous-as-hell first-time grandparents, my son was handed over to me. It was easily the happiest day of my life.

But strangely it wasn't the happily ever after I had hoped for.

I think the suddenness of it all and the buildup leading up to the moment of Atin's homecoming sent me into an adoptive equivalent of post-partum depression. Even though I had nested and saved up for a potential break from my career, nothing prepared me for actual motherhood. It was terrifying being responsible for everything that went into and came out of another human being, be it food or value systems. And since I had chosen to be a single parent, I was extra hard on myself.

Acting out of what honestly was temporary insanity, I refused help and insisted on doing all the chores single-handedly. Also, because he was adopted, I was mortified that I'd miss the umbilical signs and not understand him in my gut, that I wouldn't feel an instinct tell me if he was hungry or sleepy or in pain. So I would gawk at him all the time, trying to understand what he needed. He in turn, looked at me like a mouse looks at an eagle. The moment I would enter a room, he'd dart in the other direction right into my mother's waiting arms—who was happy to be his primary caregiver. It made me incredibly angry that my son was choosing to be with the person who actually delayed his entry into my life. I wanted to bludgeon every writer, poet, or artist who said, 'Motherhood is a beautiful, magical experience'.

It wasn't for me.

I was miserable and wept myself to sleep on so many nights. I prayed for a miracle; for some way that I could bond with my son and have him love me.

My prayers were answered, so to speak, and I was rewarded with a clinical nervous breakdown. I could no longer change diapers, give Atin his midnight feed, take him for an evening walk, or give him a bath. I wasn't allowed to do any of these tasks. What I could do was to be lazy with him, read to him, and sing to him.

It was in this phase that I saw Atin warm up to me slightly. He dared to crawl closer, and I began to enjoy being his mom. But surely enough, as my body began to recover, my mental health showed signs of deterioration and I looked like I was transforming into momzilla again. That's when my father, who had been relatively silent in our estrogen-driven drama, sat me down and said, 'Priya, the problem is that you're trying to be superwoman, but what Atin needs is a mother'.

I was stunned because what my dad was actually saying was that I had to be more like *my* mother—the one person I spent my whole life trying to be different from. But Appa was right. I was play-acting 'mommy', not *being* one, and that had to change. I realized two things that day: That my son needed me to be a parent, to put his needs before my drama, and that the only thing that differentiates a good parent from a bad one, is love—and by that yardstick, I had an excellent mother myself. Even when she made mistakes, she only ever operated out of love for me. This realization gave me the strength to turn it all around.

Today Amma, Atin, and I, are a family, since my father has passed away. Sometimes we fight, sometimes we can't stand each other, but we also love each other. Atin and I are in a good place, which really means that when his vocabulary is better, he will be telling people, 'My mother is one crazy woman—she is pushy, critical and dominating. She always wants me to do better'. Well, what can I say? I have turned into my mother, which is something that would have scared the daylights out of me a few years ago. But today I see that it's not such a bad thing after all. Having said that, I must say that I am luckier than Amma because my son sees my flaws and not only does he forgive me for them, he actually loves me in spite of them, which is more than I ever did for my mother.

Priya Ramanathan is a freelance writer in Mumbai.

Little Green Men

Michael Burns

There are some things I know, and some things I don't know. One thing I know is that I'm not a huge fan of former US President, Barack Obama. I don't know him personally and from what I've seen of him, he seems like a very cool guy to sit down and have a beer with—as does George W. Bush for that matter. Of course, don't get me wrong, I'm *absolutely* not in support of the Republican Party, the counterpart to Obama's Democrat Party, either. I'm probably against between 99 and 100 per cent of everything the Republicans stand for. With Obama and the rightward drift of the Democrats, it's more like 50 per cent that I disagree with, so I don't think that qualifies me as a diehard fan.

I'm a member of the Green Party. It was founded in 1984

and has grown to the fourth largest party in the United States. The party platform stands for economic equality, social justice, workers' rights, fair trade, responsible military action, immediate addressing of the damage we're doing to the environment, and far more accountability for corporations. There are Green parties in dozens of countries so it's not just a US thing, of course. It's part of a movement, and a movement that suggests that many of the problems in our world can be traced to the concentration of too much power in too few hands.

I really do believe in democracy—in the power, intelligence and collective wisdom of everyday people to make the decisions most important in their lives. And to me, this is the party that best matches those values.

The great thing about the Greens is that we accept all-comers, meaning that the Greens aren't an exclusive club where only the elite or well-connected are encouraged to participate. Everyone is welcome.

The bad thing about the Greens is that we accept all-comers. In other words, when you have a totally open-door policy, you get all kinds of people. Yes, you get people who are passionate, who want long-term change, and who want to make a difference, but you also get eccentrics, activists focused only on one issue, as well as people who might look a little off, or act a little strange, or smoke a little something here or there—but hey, whoever said democracy was easy? It's a messy process and learning to find common ground, even within a diverse party, is all part of the fun.

So, before I came to India, I started the local chapter of the Green Party in the cluster of towns where I lived in Massachusetts. After a few months of getting the word out, there were about ten or fifteen of us who would come to the meetings regularly, which is actually pretty good for any political steering committee. We'd exchange ideas, talk about important events and news items, and most importantly, discuss upcoming elections and who, from our group, might be interested in running for office. This was an exciting time for the Greens—several party members had won seats nationally and in the state as well. Of course, the Greens are incredibly tiny compared to the two largest parties, but you have to start somewhere. We all met about once a week.

One of our regular members was Betty.

Betty and her family owned a popular campground a few towns away from where the party met. She was an older lady, short, with silver hair, in her seventies and very sharp. Her husband was an award-winning poet and though he didn't come to the meetings, she always told us that he supported our work and that the campground was always open to us if we ever needed to hold an event. No offense at all to anyone else in our organization—they were all lovely, thoughtful and intelligent people— but what I liked most about Betty was that she was… *normal*. What I mean is that she wasn't a fanatic, nor was she eccentric. She was easy to talk to, rational, and a business owner—so she even brought the small business perspective to our group, which was great.

There was a lot on the agenda at our meetings. One of our members was running for mayor, and others were organizing petitions and demonstrations, and so we often had hours and hours of items to talk through each week. One meeting ran late one night and as I always did, since I was the organizer, I would ask if everyone was okay to get home and if anyone needed a ride. Every once in a while, someone did. That night, Betty asked if anyone was going in her direction and if they could drop her off. I *was* actually, and so I told her I would be happy to drop her home.

It was dark on the highway. The campground where she lived was secluded and you got there by taking the interstate for twenty-five minutes or so and then exiting and taking small backroads the rest of the way. People went there to get into the forest and away from any noise and traffic so it was kind of in the middle of nowhere.

Although Betty had been coming to our meetings for the last year, this was the first real chance that she and I had to talk and so it was really nice to finally get to have a proper conversation. Maybe it's just my personality, too, I don't know, but I get along especially well with older people. I just love their wisdom and perspective on things, maybe because in politics, they can appreciate political change simply because of how much life they've seen.

She and I talked about all kinds of things on that ride.

It was September and that summer had been an eventful one for me. I did an internship in another part of the country and it made a huge impression on me for many reasons. But something very unusual happened on that internship, something involving cars and the highway—something unexplainable that, even to this day, I can't fully wrap my head around. Anyway, it came to my mind because this thing that happened to me, also happened on a dark night on the road. I told Betty the story and she listened carefully and thoughtfully as she always did. I told her that maybe above all, this strange thing that happened to me opened my mind to the possibility that maybe more was out there in the world than we first thought. We can call it paranormal or whatever you want to call it, but this experience defied explanation, and so the lesson I learned was never to dismiss any phenomenon out of hand even if it seems strange and unlikely—maybe it takes something bizarre happening to you before you decide to take that approach to life. As we drove on, I could see the stars lighting up the sky, and I told her there was one exception to this new open stance of mine—which was a belief in aliens.

The US has a unique relationship with a belief in aliens. While most of the world's countries are in the single digits of percentage of the population that believes—9 per cent in Holland and 8 per cent in Sweden for example—in the US it's about 54 per cent, with nearly half of those believing that aliens are not only out there but have visited Earth at one point in our history.

Despite the numbers of my fellow Americans who believe, I told Betty that I felt really bad for people who believed in bug-eyed non-human visitors because it was obviously some kind of medical anxiety reconstituted as a nightmare about probing and abduction and so forth. Medical surgery and the possibility of feeling helpless during a procedure is something millions of people face every day, so it's not like these scenarios are coming out of the blue; they're clearly universal fears. It doesn't take a genius to realize that these anxieties have just been repackaged with the face of an E.T. put on them. I mean, if these things really existed, then why wouldn't there be a *range* of experiences with aliens, some understandably scary but others very positive and even inspiring? Instead, alien encounters were always, without fail, negative. It just didn't make sense.

Betty listened and nodded along, but at the end, cocked her head to the side and said, 'It's strange though, that you have an open mind to everything else but not this. I guess it goes against your own logic to be so closed to this.'

'Actually,' she said, 'you should be open to this, too—because they're real.'

'What do you mean?' I asked.

And for the next ten minutes, Betty described to me, in intricate detail, what had happened, but with the intensity of reading off a to-do list. On 17 December 1981, she was making breakfast for her two daughters at their home in the suburbs just outside of Chicago and was standing in front of her stove. She turned around in her kitchen and there were two figures standing there—two short grey beings with large eyes and thin limbs. Her heart almost stopped. She stood there frozen with a combination of terror and confusion as she looked at them and they looked at her. All she thought about was the safety of her daughters and she ran upstairs as fast as she could, woke them both up from a sound sleep, forced them to get dressed immediately, and told them they were late for school. It was actually a Saturday, which isn't a school day in the US, and the kids went outside in a panic, and then came back in a few minutes later, completely confused, after their Mom had calmed down.

A few years went by before anything happened again. She was alone in the house and she glanced up in the living room and this time, there was just one of them there—same expressionless face as before; just standing there looking at her.

Betty said to me, 'They were as real as me and you sitting right here in the car.'

I said, 'But, isn't it possible that you had seen one too many sci-fi movies or comic books and that this was a vivid dream that somehow got filed wrong and now you think of it as a memory?'

She said, 'I never watched sci-fi movies ever in my life. I didn't even have any idea as to what these things were; only that they were very strange, seemed intelligent and made me feel incredibly nervous. I had no reference point, no idea what to call them even, until years later when I thought I was going crazy, I did some research and found that there were other people who had had similar experiences. Maybe the strangest encounter I've had with them,' she said, 'was when one of them took me on their craft and showed me around it. It was horrifying and nauseating and confusing and the most surreal experience I've ever had.'

I was just driving and listening.

She said that back then, she had no idea how to process this and was way too embarrassed to share it with anyone until something happened five years after that initial day in 1981. Her oldest daughter, who was a teenager at this point, came to her one day and told her that she had something to tell her. She didn't know how to say it so she just came out and said it. She said that for several years she had been seeing something—some *things*— and she thought they were creatures from another planet. At this moment Betty realized that she wasn't crazy and both of them told their secrets to the rest of the family. Nobody could believe it but they found some way to accept it and although they don't talk about it much, they've all lived with this ever since.

Betty looked out the passenger's side window. She told me the whole story very matter-of-factly—not that it was rehearsed but like it was no big deal, like it was just a normal part of who she was. No drama, no special emphasis, no desperate tone to try to convince me; just dry and plain.

I kept driving and we rode in silence for a little while as I exited the highway and found the road toward the campground.

'But if aliens are around, how come not everyone can see them? There should be photos and videos and all kinds of evidence, right?' I asked.

'I don't know,' she said. 'I have so many questions too; way more than you have probably. Maybe it's like a dog whistle or ultraviolet light. These things exist even though we can't hear them or see them—maybe seeing them is like that for some reason. Maybe you have to be attuned to it or something.' In the end she had no idea why she could see and interact with them and most people couldn't.

All of what she said was processing over and over in my mind as I pretended I didn't care much. One thing was completely true: *She* believed this with absolute certainty. This woman was not making this up as far as her own personal perspective. She told it all to me as if she didn't care. She wasn't trying to convince me. She was just telling me what she had experienced. Either she was the world's greatest actor running a campground for some reason, or she was telling me what she saw as the truth. Now that leaves two possibilities. One is that she's crazy. She seems normal but can't tell the difference between what's real and unreal. And also, somehow, her daughter also shares these delusions. Or the other possibility… which I'm not comfortable thinking about.

The paved road turned to dirt and we had a short, bumpy ride to the entrance of the campground. I pulled up to the house and she gave me a big smile and one of those half car-hugs that you do and thanked me for the ride. I told her I'd see her the next week and made a U-turn to head home.

I pretended that this wasn't distressful for me, but it was. My heart was racing and the car seemed suddenly quiet. What was this all about? Why did she tell me this? What am I supposed to think? Is it possible—is it in any way possible—that what she's saying is true? Sure, nearly everything is possible. But is it probable? No. No, it's not.

But I kept thinking. What if they *are* out there and the problems that we have are things they've solved long ago—

problems of war, inequality, disease and, of course, how to travel to other solar systems? Above all, what if they've evolved a new way to communicate, which goes beyond words and beyond language and exists only through thoughts? And then it hit me. What if they can read your thoughts? What if all they need to be able to communicate with you is to be able to tell that you might believe in them?

Sweat started to build up on my forehead. My vision started to narrow as the car bounced on the pitch-black, dirt road lined with empty cornstalks on each side. What if they know right now that I might believe that they exist? And what if they're going to show themselves to me now because of that? All I kept thinking was: *I don't want to see them. I don't want to see them. I don't want to see them.* And I started repeating this to myself out loud. 'I don't want to see them. I don't want to believe. I can't handle seeing them.' And then I started crying. I'm now convinced that I had been initiated into this group of believers and now I was one of the ones who could witness them. I'm crying and shaking, with the headlights lighting just twenty feet in front of the car, desperate to get out of the middle of nowhere and home as soon as possible, or at least anywhere where there was another person who could offer instant protection from them.

I drove in terror for the next ten minutes, convinced that I was going to see something step from the side of the road and wave the car to a stop. I could swear that I could see that expressionless face taking shape in front of the car. I sat on the edge of my seat with a primal scream sitting in my throat, just waiting to come out.

Somehow I made it home that night. Nothing visited me. At least nothing I remember. I tried to forget about that night. And I've done a pretty good job of putting it into a part of my mind where it doesn't get stirred up very often.

So all these years later, do I believe or not? Actually, I don't know what I believe. I *do* know for a fact that when I'm all alone in the middle of the night, or in the early morning hours that I get up most days, I don't like the feeling of being the only person in the neighbourhood who's awake. I don't like it when there are no witnesses of any kind. When I realize that I'm completely alone, I try to find a window and walk over to it and tell myself I don't believe in them. But then a few seconds later, I say a little prayer to them and tell them I *do* believe, but in exchange for my belief, to please leave me alone.

I'm very curious about what's out there, beyond the limits of what we currently understand. But I'm also terrified of it. Somewhere, deep inside, I want to know who we are, where we come from and, most importantly, why we're here—what this whole crazy thing called life is all about. But as the saying goes, be careful what you ask for...

...you just might get it.

∿

Michael Burns is a university teacher and the director of Tall Tales.

I Hate Moonlight

Chandrima Das

Everyone wants someone special—someone who will take interest in everything they care about, someone who'll send them presents and stuff, who'll think about them all the time, doodle their name in class, talk about them incessantly, and who'll worry about them day and night. Everyone wants someone special—until they get a stalker.

Some stalkers think they're doing you a favour. They're giving you the gift of limitless attention, so how can anyone not like it? Well, I think the very word 'stalking' implies that you're *not* supposed to like it. Otherwise, it would be called 'fluffy, harmless observation time'.

I am not proud of the story I am about to tell you. I make

a lot of mistakes in it. Five, to be precise. Yes, tonight, I'm going to be Chetan Bhagat and tell you about the five mistakes of my life. I hope you take heart from them and learn from them, even if I didn't.

Most of all, I want to tell you this story not because it's entertaining, but because we live in a country and in a culture that trivializes stalking. On the Indian screen, some guy devotes himself to prove his 'love' to some woman who is clearly exasperated and completely uninterested and an audience of two-hundred people goes, 'Oh my God! That is so romantic'.

Seriously?

You actually want to be in a relationship with a person who'll throw everything away in a second for an ounce of your attention? Or, even worse, someone who will harm themselves out of a sign of supposed love for you?

'Darling, you didn't pick up the phone at work so I lopped off a toe.'

'Darling, you didn't hug me yesterday so I chopped off an ear.'

After a year, you'll find yourself married to a torso with no limbs—just like Darth Vader.

I was in my first year at IIM Calcutta and I had just landed an internship with a top consulting firm. I was manning—or personing—the reception area, and I was responsible for the phones, directing other students looking for internships as to where to go for their next interviews and so forth. And that was 'How I Met My Stalker'.

As I later found out, this was not how my stalker met me. Stalkers typically have a way of 'meeting' you long before *you* meet them.

He had an air of anxiousness around him as he came up

and said, 'Hi. This seat here seems to be empty', sitting down next to me. He sat there fidgeting a bit, occasionally awkwardly participating in the banter around the front desk that Abhishek, Hrishikesh and I had going. All I remember about him from that day was his nervousness, the fact that he made me uncomfortable for some reason, and his name.

Yes, my stalker has a name. He is a person with feelings and intelligence, who now has a great career. But I will not tell you his name. I will proceed to de-humanize him a little, just as he de-humanized me a little.

He was back the next day: Surer, better-dressed and smelling like an entire bottle of aftershave had been emptied on his head. At the end of a long, strange day, punctuated by him paying me rehearsed compliments that sounded like they came from *Men's Health* magazine, he stopped, squared his shoulders to me, looked into my eyes and said, 'I have a crush on you. A very big one.'

And then I made the first mistake in this story. I tried to use logic.

'Thank you. That's very flattering', I said. 'You've only known me for a few hours. I find it hard to understand how anyone can have a crush on someone they don't really know.'

'But I know you. I know pretty much everything there is to know about you.'

Oh crap.

'I've been observing you for a while. And I can't get you out of my head.'

Just then, Abhishek came around to the front desk and plonked himself next to me. 'Go get something to eat, CD. I'll man the desk,' he said. To this day, I wonder if he had heard what had just transpired and came in to help me, or if it was just coincidence.

I had escaped. But only for now. Little did I know then, that this was Day 2 of a story that was to be stretched over the course of the next five years.

Some days later, my friend Rajji and I were on one of our evening walks around the largest lake at the IIM Calcutta campus. Over the preceding few months, she and I had gotten into the habit of making a couple of rounds every night after dinner, discussing the events of the day. Minutes into our walk that night, I heard footsteps behind us. This didn't alarm me in particular, because Rajji and I were hardly the only fools on campus who were willing to be shat upon by birds after dinner. There would always be students taking walks around the campus at any given point in time, be it 7 in the morning or 3 in the night.

The shuffling footsteps caught up with us.

'May I join you ladies?' said a shaky, male voice.

There he was—nervous, sweaty and stammering as usual. Rajji and I exchanged glances. Her glance said, 'Why is this guy sweating so much in the middle of November?' My wide eyes silently screamed at her: *Say no, Rajji. Please say no. Be unfriendly for once, instead of the wonderful, sweet person you are. Just say it.*

Rajji said something nearly as good. She looked at him and answered his question with, 'Why?'

He said, 'Because I'd like to walk with you. That isn't a crime, is it?'

This was when I made my second mistake of the story—politeness. I said, 'Of course not. Apologies if we're being rude. Please feel free to join us.'

The three of us—an odd trio now—continued with our walk in complete silence. After one round, as opposed to our usual three or four, I muttered in a tone way too formal for me,

'I have a coursework related meeting now and, um… Rajji does, too. So we gotta run.'

He looked at me curiously and with genuine concern. 'Cutting short your walk because of me, Moonlight? It's usually longer, isn't it?'

Moonlight. A translation of my name. There it was for the first time. I've been addressed by many names by many people throughout the course of my life. The formal Chandrima, my initials CD, the affectionate Siddy, Chan or Chanda, the cuddly Chandu, the mildly theatrical Chandramukhi, and then Shamindra, the odd thing that a fifty-year-old client from Arlington, Virginia, christened me. But the literal Sanskrit translation. So seemingly appropriate. Simple. Personal.

Over the course of the next five years, I grew to hate it.

I hate Moonlight.

Ping

The IP messenger I had installed on my laptop buzzed yet again. This was a LAN messaging system popular with the Internet nerds on campus at the time. We shared links to files and inside jokes, ran web radios, broadcasted announcements, etc. It was our internal Reddit, 9gag and Twitter, all rolled into one.

The ping said I had a private message. Private messages were unusual. And unlike Gmail, unblockable. I opened it.

What's up, Moonlight?

I did not respond.

Are you angry, Moonlight?

No, I replied, *I am not angry. There's nothing to be angry about here. But you are making me very uncomfortable. Please stop.*

Is it so bad that I just want to be around you?

Now, I consider myself as someone who can see things from the other person's perspective—the burden of empathy.

It prevented me from being preemptively mean to him. After all, he had not harmed me, nor had he displayed any intention of doing so. At this point he was just being mildly annoying.

I think I understand where you're coming from. It is perfectly natural to feel attracted to someone. But the kind of behaviour you're exhibiting makes life very difficult for me. You don't even know me.

But I do. I know what you're good at and what you like. I've seen your grades. I know who your friends are. I just heard you sing fifteen minutes ago.

I froze. I *was* singing fifteen minutes ago. In my hostel room. With the door closed.

When I didn't reply for a few minutes, he pinged again.

Are you very busy, Moonlight? So busy that you can't reply to me?

I replied with the three words I had been holding back for a week now: *Stop stalking me.*

He replied immediately.

But I am not stalking you. I just have a crush on you. I don't understand why you have a problem with that. I am not even asking you to spend time with me.

Of course, he was 'right', as stalkers always are. Following me, keeping track of my activities, finding out who I hang out with, harassing me and pinging me continuously were all borne out of love.

Here, I made the third mistake in this story. I did not uninstall IP messenger. I tried reasoning with him in the beginning, explaining my position. I did this with the belief that I would not let this one annoying, persistent person dictate my decisions and my behaviour. I was a strong, independent young woman. I could totally handle a stalker with grace, humor and empathy. I would kill him with kindness. I would show him that I, too, was a person—not the mere object of his affection. He would see me as a human being, not a goddess on a pedestal. I would tell him that not every person you're attracted to is obligated to respond in kind—and that I already had someone in my life at the time. And hopefully, he would understand and back off. After all, he seemed to be an intelligent person.

As it turned out, I was an idiot for thinking this.

The pings continued. More desperate. More frequent.

My initial attempts to be rational, reasonable and to clarify my position, tapered down. At the end of four weeks of this harassment, most—in fact nearly all—of his pings started going unanswered. There were messages to tell me where he had seen me that day, pings to tell me why I shouldn't be spending time with certain male friends of mine, and even pings to tell me how I looked on certain days.

On 14 February 2009, about three months after this had started, at 2 a.m., I heard a knock on my door. Being the night owl that I am, I was awake. I had posted something odd/funny/ silly on the IP messenger, as I was often known to do. While it may seem unusual in other contexts, there's nothing odd about having a visitor at 2 a.m. when you're on campus. But, little did I know who was on the other side of the door.

He stood outside with a bouquet of flowers and a box of chocolates, sweating profusely, as anxious and nervous as the last time I had seen him, which had been the incident of the walk around the lake with Rajji. Despite pinging me up to fifteen times a day for the last three months, he hadn't gathered the nerve to meet up with me all this time; a lack of courage I was extremely grateful for, right up until this moment.

'For you,' is all he said as he stood there fidgeting nervously, arms outstretched SRK-style.

You can probably guess what's coming next. Especially when

I say that this was when I made the fourth mistake of this story. I took the box and the bouquet from his outstretched arms. I still don't know what compelled me to do it.

He smiled triumphantly.

Then I realized just what I had done. I motioned to hand the gifts back to him.

'Happy Valentine's Day,' he said, as he quickly walked away from the doorway and disappeared down the stairs. I stood there at the doorway, completely mortified by my own stupidity.

A few seconds later, my neighbour passed me by, standing there motionless and confused, on her way to the bathroom. She stopped. 'Oh wow! Who are *these* from?'

'They're from the creepy guy I had told you about. He just came and handed these to me and left.'

'Sooooo cute!' she shrieked, jumping up in pure glee. Her excitement was proportional to my sense of dread.

My acceptance of these gifts would forever be held against me. In his head, he had probably just atoned for the harassment that he had bestowed on me. Had I just endorsed his behaviour in a way? Or, at least, *participated* in some way in his apology? Would it now all be on my head? Had I just been handed a bomb and not had the sense to run at the very sight of it?

He continued to stalk me with the very same intensity until the time he graduated in March 2009. His one-sided rants would range from friendly and funny to pleading attempts at emotional blackmail.

Do you think you're too good for me? You are arrogant and heartless, and you can't see how much I suffer because of you. I can't study. I can't sleep. I am on medication. But you don't care. You wouldn't care if something happened to me, would you?

I eventually responded by writing to him and explained that

I was going to uninstall messenger and block him everywhere else—too little, too late, of course. I had earlier given up trying to convince him that I was a human. And now, I had given up my silence. He responded by calling me on my phone—numbers were freely available in the campus directory—and demanding an explanation.

We are insidiously conditioned to think that whoever externally exhibits greater signs of suffering and pain in a situation is naturally the victim. Our movies condition us to believe that the recipients of 'unrequited love' have it easy; they are selfish people who cannot see the awesome-sauce creatures their stalkers are. I was the villain. He was, somehow, the victim.

'I can't change how I feel about you. What terrible things have I done, Moonlight? Have I ever caused you any harm?' he said, stammering. His voice sounded hoarse, like he had been crying.

I had pondered over this question for a while now. When he had initially started stalking me, my ready answer to this question would have been 'No'.

But my answer had changed now.

'You have held me responsible for your feelings, a responsibility that I would like to politely decline. You are inherently selfish and lack empathy. You claim that you have feelings for me, but I have never experienced anyone to be so inconsiderate towards me. My decisions, my willingness, my consent or my lack of consent is of no consequence to you. And yet you claim that you care deeply about me. You have induced fear in me and you have made me start to look behind me when I never used to before. If your aim was to make me feel guilty about my very existence, then yes, you have nearly succeeded. But I won't let you pin your weakness and your obsessive behaviour on me. I am not responsible for you. *You* are responsible for you.'

I cut the call. I did not pick his calls thereafter.

After he graduated, the frequency of these attempts to interact died down eventually. 'Eventually', as in, over one whole year. I would sometimes get very odd anonymous emails of a stalkery disposition. I'm sure it was him even though I can't pin them on him since they were anonymous. I would *like* to believe it was him primarily because one stalker at a time is all I can handle.

After two years of complete silence, in May 2013, he contacted me again, having obtained my phone number from a mutual friend. He contacted me to tell me that he was doing fine and had been 'cured'. He hadn't 'been obsessed with me for a while now' to use his own words. He had undergone therapy and he just wanted me to know that. I welcomed his new state of being and wished him well.

My fifth and final mistake of this story.

The next day he called me again and proceeded to tell me all about how he had undergone aversion therapy using shock treatment, adding, after a pause: 'All for you, Moonlight'.

Whatever aversion therapy he had undergone clearly hadn't worked. He was back, stammering a little less, but now armed with the confidence to speak to me.

I pitched one last effort to tell him how any interactions with me were just plain bad for him. It clearly caused him problems, and at the rate he was going, he would never get over this illogical obsession. After I finished, I blocked him on my phone. He hasn't got back in touch again.

I don't feel relief, however. I have permanently turned into someone forever looking over my shoulder. I subconsciously dread picking up the phone when I get calls from unknown numbers. I wonder sometimes when the next anonymous email will drop into my inbox—and all of the baggage that comes with that.

And that leads us to the problem with this story: It doesn't have an ending. The ending of a story is about finding a way to close it, that's meaningful and satisfying. This story is incomplete. It's incomplete because the ending of this story is not in my hands. I don't have the power to end it. I don't have the power to end his obsession with me. Only he does.

And I can only hope that he has.

Chandrima Das lives in Mumbai and is an Associate Director at FSG, a social impact consulting firm.

The Skeleton

Apala Bhattacharya

It was hanging in my room. Wearing a white saree, it tapped rhythmically against the wall in the cold breeze of the night, casting long shadows on my bed and grinning back at me in the moonlight.

It was the skeleton, my roommate.

The skeleton came into our possession in the early 1990s in a desperate attempt to save my father's legacy. Dad was a brilliant doctor, or so they say. He died before I could form any clear memories of him, so their word is all I have to go by. When we, his offspring, all started showing a flair for the arts, Ma did what Indian mothers do in that situation—she sprung into damage control mode. A fully-equipped home lab was created, complete with test tubes, beakers, chemicals that smelled like dead animals, body parts in jars of formaldehyde, and yes, the real skeleton of a deceased person.

I slept in that lab. Not because we didn't have enough rooms—it was a looming, old, ancestral home and so there were many rooms—but because it was the *only* room free of pesky humans. No one ever entered the dark, smelly lab. Life happened outside of it. There, in its odd quarantine, I had the luxury of complete privacy—time froze and I could get lost in the labyrinth of my own mind. So, what's a measly little skeleton to deal with?

Mr Sen, my sister's tutor for biology, was working his way through medical school, and one evening, after he had completed a study session at our dining table, we unveiled the skeleton for his expert (or soon-to-be expert) opinion. He employed questionable forensic skills and identified the bones as such: female; approximately twenty-four years old at the time of death; unmarried (I don't know where he got *that* detail from); and cause of death—head injury. There was a crack in the skull indeed. We guessed that it was probably from a road accident, or maybe a fall.

Or maybe it was a quick blow to the head with a blunt instrument. Yes; definitely that. Let's definitely say murder. Much more dramatic.

It was my Dida (Bengalis call their maternal grandmothers 'dida'), who thought that dressing her in a saree would keep her clean. We wouldn't have to dust her, which was a good point. So they wrapped her in Dida's laal paar shaada saree (which is a traditional Bengali white saree with a red border), draped a ghomta (veil) over her head, and hung her on the hook in my room. And so, I had a lab as a bedroom, with the skeleton of a (possible) murder victim hanging for company, facing my bed, wearing a white saree, and rattling about in the dead of the night.

And I was cool with it.

Ma would make me label her body parts, count her vertebrae and locate where the organs would have been. I'd lie on the bed and stare at her, and I'd create these elaborate stories with me and the skeleton as adventurers, pirates, detectives, and even—dare I say it?—lovers. Hadn't Healthcliff from *Wuthering Heights* dug out Catherine from her grave, clung to her skeletal remains on a dark and stormy night, and taught everyone that that's how real love was supposed to be?

Clearly, while my mother was trying to turn me into a doctor, I was turning into a storyteller.

Eventually, my mother realized that we weren't going to win the school biology prize (which was named after our Dad), unless we hoped to do so with particularly eloquent poetry. My older sisters, despite much resistance, had all chosen different, non-science, academic paths, and I quickly turned out to be a lost cause.

One day, the test tubes and jars in the lab mysteriously disappeared. Taking this as a sign that my mother had given up on me, I dug out old books from my grandfather's trunks: *War and Peace, Waiting for Godot* and short stories about Russian prostitutes by Guy de Maupassant—I was ten. I populated the now-empty shelves with these books, along with the occasional Enid Blyton. It was a confusing time. The bookshelves went all around the room, starting from the floor and reaching the ceiling. Every once in a while, I would climb them like a jungle-gym and pick my book of choice to get lost in. It was bliss.

My bedroom had gone from being a lab to a library. Only the skeleton remained as evidence of my mother's feeble attempts at manipulating our future.

That's when they built her a coffin.

The coffin was specially crafted to her dimensions—the carpenter measured her out. And just to spice it up, they painted it lime green; not because Dida expressed herself through colour irony, but because that's what was left of the house paint. Always the practical one, Dida slapped a mattress on top of the coffin and it beautifully doubled up as the maid's bed. Of course, the maid never knew, which I've always felt kind of bad about. And so the skeleton stayed, as the maid's bed companion, for a good couple of years. We wondered why Ma didn't just get rid of the skeleton, but she had her plans.

A decade later, we found out exactly what those plans were.

One fine day, my mother mused aloud, 'Accha, how much does it cost to ship a skeleton to the US?'

We were moving to our new home—one without a lab. My oldest sister had married and moved to Los Angeles and had had a baby. My other sister and I were old enough and so it was a good time to leave the ancestral home and shift into a cozy apartment nearby. Most of our stuff was coming with us—but not the skeleton.

The skeleton was applying for a green card.

On careful questioning, it appeared that Ma, knowing that we were lost causes, had secretly pinned her hopes on the fact that one of us would produce an heir with a flair for science. Since my sister had married an Ivy Leaguer, the one-year old offspring of this divine union must be science-worthy, she thought. So what if the little one can barely walk? Catch 'em young, right! No better way to introduce the child to wonders of medicine than with a real, full-sized skeleton to use as a rattle.

The feasibility of shipping the skeleton was discussed at

length. We wondered about the legality of trying to ship a real skeleton with a cracked skull to distant land. Was there a statute of limitations on murder and evidence gathering? Whether the fear was legitimate or unfounded, the thought of possible jail time finally convinced my mother to abandon her grand plans of skeleton relocation.

And then she took the logical, and therefore, to us, the most shocking step—she finally got rid of the skeleton.

She sold the skeleton to a student of homeopathy for ₹1000, coffin included. Ma still laments the selling: 'I bought it for ₹5000 in *those* days, mind you.' And just like that, all traces of my one-time companion, my fellow saree-clad, deceased adventurer were gone, along with my mother's high hopes for our future and the future of generations to come.

᷎

Apala Battacharya is a copywriter and lives in Mumbai.

Vicky Donor

Maxwel Chhetry

Struggling actors are much like the sperm that Vicky, the donor boy, bequeathed on his way to national fame—only one in a million succeeds. It's an ode to Bollywood, really. So, it's strangely apt that when I decided to seriously pursue acting, I got a role in the movie *Vicky Donor*.

Someday, I want some movie to carry 'Introducing Maxwel Chhetry' in their credits. Technically, I've debuted already. Will they count *Vicky Donor* and the film *Amu*? I had precisely the same screen time in both—three and a half seconds. Needless to say, I wasn't incredibly critical to the plot. So maybe they'll ignore these blips on the radar when they finally cast me in a big, introductory role. I may even have to put up a fight about my debut status if they think my bit parts were significant. These are the hardships of stardom.

I'd shot for the movie in November 2011 when I was still living in Gurugram and doing community theatre in Delhi. One day, I'm lamenting the fact that hardly any movies are shot in Delhi, and the next day I get a call from a theatre friend that she's on the set with a crew shooting a film in Lajpat Nagar. Her sister's writing the script and it's a cracker. And, she asked me whether I would like to audition for a part in the movie.

Yes, of course.

Other than a good role, the one thing that makes an actor happy is finding a contact in the industry. Any contact. So of course, I wanted to audition. I'd *walk* to where they were, if they needed me to. A friend's sister in the crew is a big deal in this little slice of the universe. It means someone will look after you and ask for a chair for you when you get there. And if you know your contact really well, they may even offer you chai.

So I went for the audition and tried to impress the assistants. There were two of them there that day, and they looked the part. I mean, you could never mistake them for anything else. They don't look like newspeople; they don't look like advertising people; they look just like ADs with their denims, their glasses, their sweatshirts and their mandatory pens clicking in their hands. They're so perfectly cast for their roles that I wonder who auditioned *them*.

I was told they need actors for small parts in the film.

'What about the bigger parts?'

'They're cast already.'

They got into a huddle and I waited expectantly. Then suddenly, one of them turned around wielding a Handycam.

'Play a sperm donor. Ready. Go.'

'Sorry, what?' I asked.

'Play someone who's getting interviewed to be a donor,' they explained.

They quickly added that the psycho donor's been cast (I don't look psycho enough). College boy donor is set as well (not young enough). Some other varieties of donors are off the table, too. Gay donor is available though.

'Can we call him effeminate? Sounds better that way, no?' I was asked.

'Sure.'

There was also the part available of a sterile NRI who comes to the clinic with his wife, seeking a donor.

So, at best, I could play sterile, and at worst, gay. Or the other way around, actually.

Anyway, they liked my effeminate audition a lot. About the other one, either I wasn't NRI enough or sterile enough. I'll never know.

So, I was given a date and time for the shoot and all the assorted 'donors' arrived at the location. We were quite a sight, the five of us lined up on chairs. Someone came over from the set and provided the mandatory joke about us 'waiting to give it a "shot"'. We had already made our own versions of that joke long before, so we just smiled politely. There's frantic activity before any shooting starts and we realized we've been called way before time. Breakfast is a leisurely affair on a set; probably the only time everyone will get to sit around together before the day's madness overtakes everything. We were looking around nervously, the five of us, suspiciously similar to our characters. Should we just help ourselves to breakfast or wait to be told? It's just food after all. One of us decided to break the ice and we all got up to eat.

We were just about finishing when someone realized we were not in costume.

'The donors aren't in costume!' someone yelled. And then like the rattling chai cups from the caterers, the message gets passed around—the fact that the donors are not in costume. One AD yelled it to the other, and the other yelled to another, until it came back and landed squarely on the costume lady. We stood around, food in hand, looking guilty for not being ready to 'donate'.

So, off to costume and make up. While psycho donor's hair was being frazzled to make him look more psycho, he continued a conversation we were having before and told the rest of us about how we'd be foolish if we decided to move to Mumbai. He'd just spent ten years there and came back disillusioned and just about ready to give up acting. 'There's no respect for real talent,' he informed us as a big glob of gel was kneaded through his hair. After seeing that we weren't convinced, he got up in a huff from his chair, exuding psychological tension just like the director was looking for. Nothing can make an actor psycho faster than reminiscing about struggling for work in Mumbai.

College boy donor was next and as soon as he sat down, he announced that he was headed to Mumbai pretty soon, no matter what anyone said.

When it was my turn, they decided I wasn't looking effeminate enough despite the red glasses and the sparkling lip gloss they had found for me. So they called in the dress department and I was made to shimmy into an incredibly tight pink t-shirt for good measure. Then we walked over to the set together—my nipples and I.

And the shoot started.

And ended.

Just like that. Literally about six minutes later.

To the collective dismay of the five donors who'd planned to spend a whole day in front of the camera, our participation—from preparation, to being shown the door—lasted exactly half a day. Of course, no one knew what a big deal the film was going to become, grossing $9.6 million, but with a budget less than a tenth of that.

I'm not sure if college boy donor's plan worked out eventually, but two months later, I certainly moved to Mumbai. Around March 2012, the promos for the movie started on TV. There was a punchy song and everyone was grooving to it already. I used to take a rickshaw to work, and the auto guy was blaring it on his speakers. My cook listened to it on the phone while she pretended to cook. In the gym, there was a woman on the treadmill next to me who ran faster every time the song came on her screen. I even heard it on a mobile as a tai-chi class was starting. In the catchy promo, the producer himself does a cameo and that was everyone's favourite part, at least in the gym. You can literally see people slowing their moves down when the song comes on. Then the tune changes, and like factory workers in a movie, everyone goes back to their previous duties.

As it was edging closer—the debut—I was excited to get to see myself in 70mm for the first time, though this was my second movie part (I didn't see the first one in a cinema). Maybe I'll never get a meaningful part in a full-length film, but at least seeing myself on the big screen was off my bucket list. And, believe it or not, I was nervous about my four-second cameo. I wished my wife was around. I would have liked to have her next to me.

Finally, the next month when the film released, I was super thrilled about the premier, but then I was told by my AD friend that a separate screening for the cast and crew was on just before the real premier: No guests and just one ticket each. 'It's okay. I don't have anyone to take,' I told him. He looked at me with a combination of understanding and pity. I was ashamed.

But obviously, I got myself to PVR Juhu where they had scheduled the event. Even for a small budget film with an uncertain future, it had attracted quite a crowd. The goatee-twins from *Roadies* were there (apparently they were friends of the lead actor from his TV days) and a smattering of C-list celebrities, the kinds that get mobbed in Jamshedpur but no one bothers about them here in Mumbai. My date was caramel popcorn—it was my comforter and provider of solace. I waited for the movie to start.

And it started—opening credits... heart is racing... catchy song... names that aren't mine... more catchy song. And then...

Just over nine minutes into the movie, I saw myself. For those few seconds, there was nothing in the frame but me. I dominated that big hall with its 150 occupants. It was my face on the screen everyone was watching and it was my voice that everyone was listening to. Pure me, with no distraction, no background score, no extras in the picture. I nearly choked on my popcorn. It was a comic scene and there was some laughter. Maybe thirty-five people laughed, I thought. And then I was gone. Just like that.

I slid down my seat to avoid the incoming stares, but realized there was no point. No one was looking for me in the dark. Everyone was glued to the film. It was captivating, funny, witty, well-executed, and my part was over. It was going to be a runaway success, I predicted, and when the closing credits started rolling, I left the theater solo, just like I'd entered.

What do people do after they see themselves on the screen for the first time? Party with friends? Go dancing? Drinking?

Should I go get myself a victory cocktail? I decide maybe a drink to soak it all in was a good idea. But at the moment of decision, I walked right past the bar. I couldn't bring myself to walk in. There's something sad about celebrating alone. And I was not feeling sad.

Instead, I found myself walking up to the rock beach in Versova. Even though I was not feeling down, I was seeking out the solitude of the sea and its grandeur. It would be a fitting end to a grand start of a grand plan. I sat myself down on a rock and that was when it hit me—the big joke—that all struggling actors are like Vicky Donor's sperms: One in a million will succeed. And I thought to myself: *As sure as I'm sitting here now, replaying my four seconds of fame, imagining if there is, in fact, fourteen minutes and fifty-six seconds left for me, surely there are thousands of other people, all across the world, from Los Angeles to Mumbai, doing the same thing.*

Am I mad to think that I can beat these odds? I don't think so. It's a dream. And dreams aren't supposed to be logical. It's not embarrassing to want something and to take a step towards it, even if it's as small as a grain of sand.

And I laugh a small laugh to myself. There's no fear of being mistaken for mad. The sea is huge.

It swallows everything.

Maxwel Chhetry is a stay-at-home dad, a screenwriter and runs a theatre-based training company in Mumbai.

Electric Socket Girl

Stephanie Zimmerman

Back in April 2015, I did my first Vipassana meditation course. For those of you who know and for those of you who don't know, a person's first Vipassana course is usually what it was for me—a ten-day retreat in almost complete silence, with no distractions. So that means no phones, no tablets, no laptops, but it also means no books, no writing; not even taking notes. And when I say it's a silent retreat, that means no talking, of course, but you're not even supposed to make *eye contact* with your fellow meditators.

So, for ten days, it's just you, alone with yourself, trying to meditate for no less than ten hours a day. And it's tough. Forget about ten whole hours, if you're not used to it, try just for ten *minutes* to focus only on your bodily sensations and see how your mind runs. Now, multiply that by six, then that number by ten. That takes you to ten days.

I never expected to do a silent meditation course. I'm too practical. I'm the kind of person a friend would ask to manage their retirement fund or plan their budget vacation or perform minor surgery on their pet or sick child. All my life, I've been focused on being responsible and the best. I was top of my high school class, I had a 4.1 GPA at a top university and I scored in the 98th percentile on the exam Americans take to go to medical school. For a time, it seemed to pay off—I had a fancy degree, a new job with potential, and even a boy. I felt like all of the important checkboxes of life success were quickly being marked off, as if my life were finally reaching a point of symmetry.

And then...

Boy and I broke up after three years—and I didn't take it well. He was my first boyfriend and also my best friend and it felt like a huge, double loss. And then soon after, the job with potential that I had moved abroad for, turned out to be a disappointment; so much so that after a year and half of sticking with it, I just had to leave, without another job or really any sort of life plan. And, as I sat in my room in the northern suburbs of Mumbai, I felt lost and defeated. I didn't know how to move forward.

But I knew I should be doing *something*, and my inability to do anything made me panic, nonstop. Every morning, I woke up and my breath was too shallow, my heart too fast, and I had this constant list in my mind of every wrong decision I had made. This list followed me throughout the day and into my sleep. And I felt completely incapable of controlling it. I don't think I'm alone in this. If you look it up, a study from Harvard in 2010 showed the average human brain spends 47 per cent of waking time thinking about the past and the future. I might be above the average on this, but we're all doing it.

During this time of panic, in the last month at my job, I happened to have lunch one day with my colleague, Kritika, who I'd heard, had done a meditation retreat. She's a person who works nonstop and who's currently in business school—so certainly not a stereotypical meditator—but she had such good things to say about her retreat. So, she gave me the name of a centre, and I just went ahead to the website, signed up before I could talk myself out of it and set off one month later. It just so happened that her retreat was Vipassana. If it had been some other sort of meditation, I would have done that, too. Even after talking with her, I barely knew a thing about Vipassana and didn't look into it any further before going. It would work or it wouldn't but I had to try something. So I went and I meditated silently for ten days, as strange and unlike me as it sounded.

I had an urge to run away the very first moment I got there. I was crammed into this tiny cabin with three other women and slept on a mattress so uncomfortable that it was only mildly preferable to sitting for the endless meditation. The bathroom was infested with monstrously big and hairy spiders, about the size of my palm. And everywhere, there were signs commanding me to 'Be Happy' with smiley-faced exclamation marks.

I hated them.

Yes, like everyone, I wanted to 'Be Happy', but I hated that they made me feel like it was some simple on-off switch that I could control just like that. Actually being happy felt like anything but simple.

In addition to this, the schedule was exhausting. I, for one, wasn't leaping joyfully out of bed at 4.00 a.m. when the gigantic gong rang, or skipping to the meditation hall for the eight daily one to two hour sessions, or relishing the fact that my last meal— actually it was technically called a snack—was at 5.00 p.m.

But, as uncomfortable as these things were, what really made me shudder was the moment I left my taxi on arriving and viewed my first fellow meditator. He was pinch-faced, very pale and he was trying to grow dreads, but he just looked like he was in a constant state of electrocution. And all I could imagine was him spending his days sitting in the dark, sticking his fingers in electrical sockets. Somehow, he totally encapsulated the true horror of this place. And I wanted to run away from him back to my taxi and beg the driver to 'Please take me to the nearest Starbucks' so that I could be with pretty-looking people again.

However, luckily for me, the next person I saw was a very sweet-faced, respectably-groomed woman, around my age and I just sighed, thinking: *Thank God, a normal-looking person, just like me.*

Super embarrassing, but true.

Within a day, I was no longer Stephanie but a set of numbers: F-22 for my bed and seat in the cafeteria; C-003 for my seat in the hall; and 75 for my bunker in the pagoda.

Like Andy Dufresne at Shawshank, I was stripped of my outer identify but that didn't stop my inner thoughts that normal, hard-working, driven people didn't do things like this. I would think to myself: *Serious people don't sit around pretending to feel things; they actually do things.* And then I would think about how I actually spend most of my time doing 'things', such as tapping on keyboards, reading about what other people do, and flipping back and forth between Gmail and Facebook. Um… yeah.

Clearly, I wasn't the most productive person. But I felt even less productive sitting in that hall because it was so boring and so tiring to be asked to sit for two hours focusing only on the sensation of my breath, and then asked to do the same thing for another hour, and then another two hours, and, by this point, after five hours of meditation, it was only 11.00 a.m. Oh God! And then there was still the afternoon and evening to get through. My back felt like burning rocks were slowly trying to bore out; my neck felt like it would split in two; and my arms and legs felt like the muscle was about to slide off the bone. And my mind. My mind felt like an addict, shrieking at me to let it take away the physical pain by shooting up with memories and fantasies. Because, when my mind got to wander, an hour of agony passed like *that*. Wandering was the easy way out.

And I despised the people around me, including 'electric socket man', who seemed so serene and most annoyingly, upright, in his meditation. There were also two 'blanket boys', always in the hall on time with their heads and bodies perfectly covered. Then 'vampire girl', with biker boots who even *walked* perfectly straight, throwing her shoulders back and flexing her neck each time before she sat down like a champion fighter. And then there was me, huddling in as close to a fetal position as I could get while still trying to maintain a semblance of semi-straightness.

And so, I spent the first three days avoiding meditation. I started skipping the 4.30 a.m. sessions and left the hall early for almost every other one. When I *was* in the hall, I did everything but concentrate on my breath; I made a twenty-something-item-long list of goals to pursue once I finally got out of that prison and back to my real life. I *did* like the no talking. I liked that no email or phone call or chat or SMS could throw off my day. I liked that break. But I hated the meditation itself. I thought it was so stupid to be asked to do this for ten hours a day;

maybe, for a few hours, yes, I could muster up the mental effort to really put some concentration toward *that*, but ten was an inhumanely, unreasonably exhausting waste of time that I knew could be put to far better use.

The only thing that motivated me to give a bit of effort was S.N. Goenka. Maybe you've heard of him, but basically he can be called the founder of modern Vipassana. Each night of the course we watched one of his videos. I didn't want to listen; by 7:00 p.m., I was always completely focused on my pain and wanted back support significantly more than listening to someone who looked like an Indian Santa Claus without the beard, give a meandering lecture filled with lots of circular fables. I mostly tried to tune him out, but sometimes, in spite of myself, his words—even the simplest of phrases—cut through. On the first night he said, 'One has to live in the present. How can you live in the past? The past is gone forever. You cannot buy back the moment that has gone away. You cannot buy back the past and relive it, given all the dollars in the world. And future is future. You cannot predict it. You have to live in the present.'

You cannot buy back the past and relive it, given all the dollars in the world. I kept repeating this to myself, because, duh, it was true, but I'd basically lived my whole life doing exactly the opposite. I had a very romantic sense of the past—that the past was what *made* me and, therefore it should be revered and, almost like an idol, continually worshipped in my mind with as much detail as possible so that it was never forgotten. And I thought of letting go as losing myself. Who would I be without my past? Who would I be if I hadn't been a lonely misfit growing up? Who would I be if I hadn't buried my social anxieties in studying? Who would I be if I hadn't found a person to make me feel normal? Who would I be if I hadn't felt abandoned by this same person? We all carry our own packages of grief. I felt broken by mine and, honestly, I liked feeling broken. How comforting it was to be able to say that all that was wrong was because this or that had happened to me; to just reach back to the past, to that person or to that event that had made me a victim. It felt impossible to give that comfort—that set of excuses—up.

Over the next few days, I still left the hall early. I still mostly tried to ignore Goenka. And sometimes I actively rebelled. A few days in, we got our individual cells in the pagoda and a cell is exactly what it sounds like: A little, bare room with a door and a tiny window up near the ceiling and one cushion on the floor for you to sit and meditate on. But the first thing I did was a big no-no and I knew it—it was even written on a prominent list of infractions. It's incredibly scandalous but… I laid down *directly* on the floor. I know what you're thinking: *Wow*.

But sometimes, I stopped faking and really did try.

Day 4 was the first day that I stayed in the hall for an entire two-hour session. That day, the focus was on sensation throughout the entire body. The previous days, the focus was on breathing and on the sensation of only your upper lip. That had been preparation for the real thing: Vipassana.

Now, I have a favour to ask of you, just to give you an incredibly tiny taste of meditation. If you don't do it very often (or ever), let's try it. After you finish this paragraph, please close your eyes, sit with your back completely straight, palms on your knees, be still, and clear your mind for ten full seconds. If you want, you can move your awareness from the top of your head, down your body, to your toes. Or it's also completely fine just to sit and focus on any sensation that comes to you.

Ready?

So, if you're into position, we'll begin with the words of Goenka: 'Observe objectively whatever reality manifests itself, any sensation that you experience. It might be tickling, tingling, itching or burning. It might be scratching, warming, prickling or paining. Whatever the sensation, observe it with perfect equanimity, remembering that in time, every sensation arises and passes, arises and passes, arises and passes.'

Now, I don't know about you, but when I tried to do this for two hours, mostly what I experienced was the early stage of a massive headache. But I tried a little more each day, and for one entire session on Day 4, I let my mind follow Goenka's voice as he guided us through each body part, from the top of the head to the toes. I felt electrical bursts of tingling across my face; I felt my hair blowing against my neck; I felt a burning between my shoulders; I felt soft pin-pricks in my foot as it fell asleep. And after that session, for the first time, I left the hall optimistic, thinking that maybe I was capable of practising something near actual Vipassana.

On Day 5 we were asked to not move our legs or arms during the day's one hour sittings. Just saying it doesn't sound that bad, but let me tell you, trying not to move for one full hour is incredibly painful, especially the first time you try to do it. On my first attempt, I gave up after forty-five minutes, thinking to myself: *This is stupid. Forcing yourself to experience this amount of pain is irrational. I don't care that this is supposed to make me happy. I don't care that 80 per cent of the people in this room seem happy doing it. I'm ten thousand miles from happy right now.* But a few hours later on that fifth day, during the next session, I told myself: *You signed up for this because your life wasn't working. For school, work, love, you said you were the hardest-working person in the world. You said you would do anything. You thought sitting around like this was for the weak anyway, so how are you of all people giving up so easily?*

So, I let my legs go numb from the thighs downward, even though I loathed the thought of those lifeless blood sacks. I let my hands grip my knees and shake hysterically. I willfully invited self-deception again and again, saying: *Just one more time, one more body scan up and down, and then, if you really can't take it, you can give up.* And just as my mind responded: *Really? Not this time; this is it; I can't do it for one more second,* Goenka's sweet voice came on, signalling the end.

On the morning of Day 8, I couldn't stop myself from crying, which was embarrassing in a space where I had no space. My mind was on *him*. It was always on him. Throughout the whole experience, 95 per cent of the memories and fantasies: Him and us. Memories that I didn't even know I had, were popping out. Some feminist I was. School, jobs, friends; I barely gave them a second thought. But a boy; he had my full attention. Why him? Because, on the first night he came over, he poked his finger gently into my stomach, saying, 'You've got a soft, gooey, marshmallow centre'. What a song to my serious, studious self. That's all that I had actually wanted, more than all the As and acceptance letters in the world, to be seen for who I actually was—sweet, sensitive, hopeful. And I thought he was the only person who could see that. So, what an incredible loss once he was gone.

Eventually, still crying, I fell asleep. When I woke up, my face looked like a wreck, but I felt unexpectedly light, in a way that I had not felt for months, and barely feeling the sad, obsessive thoughts about him. Instead, I was just mostly thinking about how eager I was to meditate again. And what I started to realize then was that while my package of grief might be with me for life, while I might always regret how that relationship ended, and while I might always wonder about the words said and unsaid on both sides, the overwhelming sadness I felt around that regret could, in fact, be temporary, and I could actively focus on making it pass. And in that way, rather than being led by this package from the past, I could start leading my own life, building something new.

On Day 9, I had one meditation session where I flowed. It felt like effortlessly running warm water up and down my body, my skin pleasantly vibrating at each touch of water. I felt capable of spending hours like that—smoothly, easily, contentedly pulsating. My heart was beating; my lungs were breathing; I was alive in that moment, *that* moment—*that* moment; not some moment in the past, not some moment in the future—and it felt amazing.

Since the meditation course ended, I've meditated for one hour a day. Now, I'm not trying to walk the Noble Eightfold Path to becoming a buddha. Frankly, the thought of being *that* pure scares me. Mostly, I'm just trying to calm the daily paralysing anxieties, and to see if, for at least one hour a day, I can be completely in the present. What I've come to understand is that the past is part of me and I don't want to forget it and I don't want to hate it, but I don't need to be defined by it. And what I like when I meditate is that I get to hear myself in the present, saying: *This is who you are. This is what you want right now. You are okay.*

Stephanie Zimmerman works on operations at a startup and lives in New York City.

The Entrepreneur's Credo

Yogesh Upadhyaya

If anyone reading this has ever started a business, been around others who have started a business, or dreamed of starting a business one day, then maybe this will strike a chord with you.

The first thing about being an entrepreneur is that you do not say no to business. When a potential client asks if you can do performance attribution against six indices, you say yes with a lot of confidence. Then you run back to the office, all the way figuring out how you are going to break the news to the delivery team that you have just signed off on their lives for the next few months. You mentally practise arguments for different members of the team:

'Sunil, instead of flying to visit your parents, why don't you call them over? A fortnight of you all living together in your one-room flat will bring all of you closer.'

'Rahul, three-day, super-quick honeymoons are the norm nowadays. Experts believe that it helps sustain the excitement of a marriage for a longer time. I'd think about it if I were you.'

'Preeti, after your baby is born, we'll get broadband installed at your home. When she wakes you at night and you can't get back to sleep, you'll have something to do.'

Okay, the last one was a bit of an exaggeration. But only a bit.

A corollary to not saying no is that you are always projecting yourself as something bigger than you are—like a puffer fish that blows itself up when it sees an enemy; or a cobra that stands up on its tail; or kind of like a Pomeranian dog. Have you visited someone who has a Pomeranian? As soon as you ring their doorbell, this cute little, long-haired mutt will come to the door and start yapping. When you step in, it will run all around your ankles, continuously yapping. The tiny little thing is trying to increase its size, trying to look ferocious.

It is very similar to start-ups. When prospective clients ask you when you were founded, you reply, 'It has been slightly less than two years' when actually it's been a year and one week since the *thought* of starting a company first came to your mind. When asked how many people work with you, you add up the total number of people to ever come in contact with the company including the people who come in once a month to do your accounts, clean the office, deliver pizza or chai, and even the postman who delivers mail in your neighbourhood. Then you multiply that number by at least one and a half, in case you forgot anyone. So again, like a small dog, you try to make yourself look bigger and more ferocious. Unfortunately, people think you are *cute*, not ferocious.

As an aside, I understand that this tendency to exaggerate

is prevalent in dating, too. OkCupid, an online dating site based in the US, did an analysis of the profiles of their members and found that the heights of men and women are a couple of inches higher than in the general population. Hmmm... So, five-feet four-inches became five-feet six-inches, and so on. The tendency was especially prevalent around socially significant heights. So, all men with a height of five-feet ten-inches and five-feet eleven-inches, became six feet. I understand that this is not restricted to just height and there is rampant exaggeration about other anatomic characteristics as well. As for me fortunately, when it comes to dating, I don't have this challenge. I am exactly six-feet tall, and not the five-feet ten that it appears at a distance.

Anyway, to the story.

I co-founded and ran a software product and services company for ten years in the late 1990s and early 2000s. We started in two rooms in a two-story bungalow in Sunder Nagar, Kalina, in the northern suburbs of Mumbai. Many of our clients, including the biggest one—ICICI Bank—were based in the Bandra Kurla Complex, only ₹8 away by rickshaw. The bungalow was surrounded by other residential buildings occupied mainly by South Indians and every morning you could hear the sounds of pressure cooker whistles accompanied by the smell of sambhar bubbling away. Wooden boards ran along the wall in the rooms and served as desks. The tiny kitchen was converted into the 'leadership' room, where all three partners of the firm squeezed in. As the company expanded, our landlord converted the stilt parking spaces just outside into additional rooms by installing plywood walls and air conditioners.

About a year after we started, we landed a client in the US. Craig Hartman was a sixty-year-old entrepreneur from just outside of Chicago who we connected with on the Internet. After a few months of doing assignments remotely, my partners and I decided that the business relationship could grow much more. We put together the money to send me to Palatine, a suburb in northern Illinois, to meet him. Fortunately, one of my cousins lived not too far from Craig's workplace.

On the day of the appointment, my cousin dropped me at Craig's office address. The two-story building was in a quiet neighbourhood and was surrounded by offices of lawyers, dentists and accountants. The only trash on the roads was a few fallen leaves—it was the beginning of autumn. When I stepped inside, I noticed that the door was made of wood—solid, respectable wood; no particle board or aluminium there. I noticed how you could actually hear yourself think and I admired how much space each of the people working in the office had. In other words, it was a typical US office in a typical US neighbourhood.

Craig and I hit it off very well in person. The two of us discussed how we could add new modules to his products—modules that his programming team did not have the bandwidth to build. I could see fulfilling work *and* dollar-denominated revenues for our baby company. Additionally, it was clear that the projects would be a great learning experience for our team and, perhaps most importantly, Craig would be a fun person to work with. He was an entrepreneur with thirty years of experience, with nearly a fourth of the US banking industry as his clients through one connection or another. He was open to new ideas and did not worry too much about working with people who were literally halfway across the world. The trip was a success…

…Except, there was a small problem. Throughout the day-long meeting, Craig kept apologizing for his office. He did not like the fact that it was based in an area where the others were dentists, for example. His was an analytical software company, he added, 'For

God's sake'. He talked about the clinic next door and I thought of the laundry hanging from the clothesline in the houses next to our place. He was unhappy about the finishing and detailing of his wooden interior while I mentally compared the perfectly painted walls with the damp, mouldy and blistered walls in ours. Most of all, he complained about the lack of space, all the while sitting in his cabin that was as big as the hall of the 1 BHK house I lived in, in Vakola. We would easily have accommodated ten programmers in that room. As he complained, I mentally removed the heavy wooden desk from his room and put up three-feet-wide wooden desks along the walls: Twelve programmers, not ten. Easy.

And of course, I did not let on that his office and his neighbourhood were ten times cleaner, a hundred times quieter and a thousand times more professional than where our office was. My face did not reveal my thoughts. If I remember correctly, I kind of agreed with him in ostensible solidarity: 'Yes, Craig, your office really could use a little work.' Not in these exact words but you know what I am saying. That, after all, is the entrepreneur's credo.

Over the next two years, our business relationship grew. He would give us new projects and we would execute them. We had weekly calls to monitor progress and discuss issues. We would talk about the latest in the budgeting world, about how AJAX could be used to make the system more responsive, and about how we were using the latest in application server technology to ensure load balancing. Once in a while, in these calls, Craig would express his desire to come visit us in India. We were always reflexively enthusiastic but would point out that monsoon was the worst time to visit Mumbai. Or that, if he happened to suggest a visit in summer, nobody came to

India at that time as it was too hot. If he insisted, or suggested a particularly decent time to come, we would tell him that we had just begun planning a trip to the US.

Craig must have thought that it was odd that there were pretty much only two seasons in Mumbai—monsoon and summer—because three years after we started working together, he told us that his good friend Larry was visiting Mumbai and he would be coming with him. He had already booked his tickets. Once I realized that it was fait accompli, I told him that we were 'thrilled, just *thrilled*', that he was coming to Mumbai.

Why did we worry about our office so much? We were very proud of the work we did and thought of ourselves as a world-class company with world-class clients. By Mumbai standards, our office was actually okay. But that was the nub of it: It was okay *only* by Mumbai standards (not even Delhi standards). How could you explain to someone else what those standards are? How do you explain stilt parking spaces boarded up with plywood walls that weren't even painted? How do you explain the vicious dog Sheru that was tied up just inside the main gate—a dog that was a grotesque combination of German Shepherd and many other assorted breeds and who bit anyone who went anywhere near it? How do you talk about multiple linear regression and multithreading when the person serving tea—Mama—is a stick-thin seventy-year-old man with just a couple of teeth, who routinely moves around, clad only in a *dhoti*? In short, how do you explain India to a person who has never visited any developing country in his life?

Our three partners had an emergency meeting the next day. Our ten-by-eight-feet executive leadership room that was smaller than the bathroom in Craig's office was converted into a war room. A campaign was designed on the four-by-three-feet white board that took up almost all the empty space.

On our recommendation, Craig booked himself in ITC Grand Maratha Sheraton. He was landing late at night and we told him that the Grand Maratha Sheraton was next door to the airport. This is true. What is not so true was the other thing we said: That our office in Kalina was really far from the hotel and he would end up wasting a lot of time in travelling there. This was all before Google Maps—the world was a trusting place then. We suggested to Craig that the traffic in Andheri was really, really bad and so we would have all our meetings in a conference room in the hotel and, if there was time and because he insisted, we would do a trip to the office on the last day in the afternoon 'when the traffic was light'.

So, for two mornings and two afternoons, different guys from our office would land up at his hotel for our meetings. The story was that we were coming directly from our homes or going there after the meeting so we were saving a lot of time. In the evenings, we went to different restaurants in the city for dinner. We went to the Taj once and once to Olive in Bandra. We would look the other way whenever we drove past the Kalina turning on the Western Express highway; our office *just* out of view. Both evenings, we reached the turning in less than fifteen minutes.

Day 3 was the last day of his trip. I had reported to the war room that the meetings had gone really well. The evening dinners had also been successes but now the visit to the office could not be avoided. We had deliberately kept a very early engagement in the evening. After a very heavy lunch and a slow coffee, we got in the car at around 3 in the afternoon. I had told Craig that sometimes, once in a while, if you were lucky, you got light traffic around that time.

Unfortunately that day, we were lucky.

The traffic was very light. Even the under-construction Andheri flyover, usually good for at least twenty minutes of chaos, took us only five minutes to get through. In all, we took the 'direct' route from Andheri to Kalina, the 'best' way being via Mahim, Dadar and the Bandra Kurla Complex. Despite the wildly unnecessary tour, Mumbai resolutely refused to participate in our deception. Forty short minutes later, we were at the office.

Sheru barked viciously when we entered, straining at his leash. Mama gave us a toothless grin. And, as we had prepared in the war room, all our employees, all forty-five of them, came out to welcome our guests. They were dressed in kurta pajamas and sarees, as we had shifted the traditional day by seventy-two hours. Craig and Larry were garlanded with thick marigold malas, red tikkas were put on their foreheads and plates with lit lamps were rotated in front of their faces. We would have arranged for shringa—the Maharashtrian trumpets—if we had found a place to source them from.

The aarti and the slow introductions worked and it was nearly half an hour later when Craig, Larry and my two partners sat down for coffee in the war room. I stood in the doorway—there was no room for five chairs. Throughout the short coffee session, Craig had a dazed look on his face. He was not commenting or even looking around the small room. There was no danger that the white board would show any traces of the plan—he was not looking. Maybe it was the 'long' drive from Andheri, maybe the jetlag was really kicking in, or maybe we had succeeded in our attempts to bamboozle him.

I doubt if it was any of the three reasons, however. I think Craig knew exactly what was happening and was trying hard to control his laughter. He was an entrepreneur himself and he knew what it was to be a Pomeranian dog barking bravely at creatures much larger than itself.

He understood the entrepreneur's credo.

ᔕ

Yogesh Upadhyaya is a serial entrepreneur with start-ups in the for-profit and non-profit sectors.

The Fourth Wall

Avinash Verma

My friend Ajitesh, an amazing stage actor from Mumbai, invited me to his play at Prithvi Theatre in Juhu a few years ago. I love all kinds of performances: movies, TV, stand-up, improv and, of course, I love going to plays. I crave the thrill and electricity of a live show, and I can't help but imagine me being up there as well. Perhaps what I love most is the fourth wall, the term for the end of the stage where our normal, everyday existence ends and the reality of the stage begins—actually separated by just a few inches, but in our imagination, worlds apart.

I went, like I usually do, with sufficient time in hand. It was a cool evening in January and it was very pleasant to sit and wait for the queue to form. I bought a ticket, grabbed a copy of the upcoming calendar for the month and found myself a seat. I sat on the bench where the line starts, enjoying the solitude and flipping through the schedule looking for faces I might know, parts I dreamt of playing one day, and highlights to scribble down in my day-planner.

Just ahead of me there was a gentleman wearing frameless spectacles, probably in his sixties, and not more than seventy-five. He turned towards me and asked, 'Are you a regular at Prithvi?' And that's how our conversation started. This older man was visiting his native India on a business trip. His whole family had moved to Kenya for work and no one he knew was now left in Mumbai. He told me about each of them in detail, and the two of us almost became friends at this point. Instead of the more common 'Uncle', I started calling him 'Uncle ji'.

The gates opened and we stood up to get in the theatre and grab our seats. If you've been to Prithvi, you know that seating is on a first-come, first-served basis and the best place to watch a play would be from the third or fourth row, centre. As soon as the tickets are checked at the door, people rush to grab those seats. It's superb 'people-watching' to see everyone rushing but still trying to maintain their dignity as they subtly elbow toward those spots. It's all smiling, giggling, talking among friends, pretending to be glued to their mobiles, acting like they don't care where they get to sit—acting cool. But everyone's focused on how to grab those amazing seats. Uncle ji knew that his best chance was to stick with a veteran, someone who knew these dark waters.

Someone like me.

We made it to the fourth row. I offered for him to sit in the very centre and took the seat to his left. Next to Uncle ji were two old aunties. Maybe it's mean to say, but they looked like South

Bombay snobbish aunties, wearing pearl necklaces as white as their hair. They were also wearing matching designer chappals. But I really shouldn't complain, because one of the things I like about Prithvi is that there are usually all kinds of people from different backgrounds at the performances, something pretty rare in this divided city. Little by little, it started to fill up while I suggested to Uncle ji what plays he should watch. Also, I invited him to one of my improv shows, after which I wrote down the information regarding the show: venue, my name and my email ID, on a piece of paper, and gave it to him. Soon, the house was packed. It was about time for the show to start.

Being a performer myself, mostly a character actor, this is always the most exciting part—the anticipation at the start, the nervous tension in the air, the curious eyes scanning the stage for how it will all begin. It's part of the thrill that makes anyone involved in the theatre feel like their time and effort is well spent. I always get a little nervous, wanting the last few late-comers to quickly get in their seats so no one's distracted at all. I love those first moments.

The lights went down. My friend Ajitesh crossed the stage and sat next to a guitarist and a drummer, on stage right. The band started playing and along with them, my friend sang a beautiful classical raga as the lights slowly came on, like a sunrise. I have heard him sing before, but this was different. He was amazing. His technique was of a well-trained artist, but he still had the freshness and spirit of a young person exploring his craft. He smoothly and seamlessly sung the most difficult parts. Everyone in the house, with occasional wows, waahs and claps, echoed my thoughts. Everyone's eyes were glued to the stage and so were mine. My friend had done his job and done it magnificently, and the audience rewarded him with a big applause.

Next, the first scene of the play started. I was watching closely, listening, analysing, and hoping for something that would grab my interest even more. Suddenly, in the middle of the second scene, an unusual light from my right disturbed me. It was Uncle ji—with his iPad. I hate when people work on their phone or tablets while a performance is on. It can obviously break the illusion of the stage and can shatter the atmosphere everyone has worked so hard to build. Yet, of course, all of us have seen people checking, replying, or—even worse—*talking* on the damn phone during a performance. It's still pretty incredible to me; even though, unfortunately, it's very common. I ignored this Uncle. Yes, 'Uncle'. The bond of friendship was now broken— he was 'Uncle ji' no more.

He put his iPad down but I didn't look over—even my reflexes were angry.

I focused my attention on my friend on stage who was jumping and singing, and the rest of the actors who were in formation, dancing around him. Just then, I heard a sound from my right. It was one of the old, snobbish aunties.

'Excuse me, excuse me.' I just sighed and shook my head. First him, and now her. I knew these ladies were going to be trouble. I kept looking forward, but I heard her again.

'Excuse me! Hello?'

Uncle was completely leaning on her, kind of falling over on his back towards them, with his hands in a weird position, almost as if he were holding a bow and arrow. His face was crooked and his body was shaking. It took me a second to realize he was having a seizure. I half stood up and immediately held his hand with my left, supporting his back with my right.

Meanwhile, the other aunty started mumbling, 'What's happening to him? He was watching something on this.' She was holding the iPad.

I saw a picture of a little girl on it, then I turned to one of the aunties, knowing the play was about to come to a screeching halt, and said, 'He is experiencing a seizure; let me help him. Please move a bit to the side so that I can place his legs on the seat.' I shouted, 'IS THERE A DOCTOR IN THE HOUSE? THIS MAN NEEDS A DOCTOR.' And the lights went on.

I looked at Uncle who was looking directly at me, as if saying: *Help me, somebody.*

Maybe the shock of the whole thing just took everyone by extreme surprise because the audience was frozen. The man's body was also frozen, and with no one moving an inch and the aunties playing with the iPad, it was left to me to do the heavy lifting. With my right hand still supporting his back, I lifted his legs with my other hand. It was hard to put him down because his body was resisting it. I tried pushing him down so that he could lie straight on his back with his head facing the ceiling. In the movies, this always seems to be the best position—at least for the lighting. But if anyone knows anything about medicine, this is the completely wrong position for someone who is experiencing a seizure.

I had no clue about it at the time. Uncle was resisting all this because he knew that I was positioning him wrong. In an epileptic seizure, a person can lose access to air and drown in his/her own fluids, and me, trying to make him lie down with his back straight, and in line with his neck, was making it worse. I realized this when after what seemed like forever, a man rushed towards us and shouted, 'No, no. Sideways—make him lie sideways.' I immediately turned him sideways and Uncle spat out. I moved a step back and froze. The man who had shouted, looked at me and said, 'It's okay. I'm a doctor.'

Another man from behind my right moved me away, 'I'm a doctor, too.' Suddenly, I was very thankful for any and all rich snobs at Prithvi.

From my left, one of the old aunties was insisting I make Uncle smell her designer chappal, claiming she knew for sure it would help. The other aunty had a small container she took out from her purse and started applying some kind of yellow powder to Uncle's feet. 'Baba's Vibhuti,' she said.

I was numb. I could see and hear, but not understand. I even held the chappal for a second, about to stick it into the growing pile around Uncle, but dropped it. One of the doctors was now searching the old man's pocket for a mobile. He found a piece of paper.

'I found something,' he said. 'A name and address.' It was the details about my show and my email ID.

'Um, that's my show info. I invited him—that's my ID.'

'Do you know him?' the doctor asked.

'No, not really. He's just a nice uncle I met outside.'

The doctor looked like a swami wearing a formal dress, 'I'm a heart surgeon,' he said and started arguing with the other doctors. I was watching them closely. Most of the comments were helpful, but some people just started talking about themselves, not about the man who needed help. Two more doctors had joined in, making a total of four doctors arguing with each other regarding procedures and techniques that should be used to save Uncle.

Suddenly, I hated the Prithvi rich snobs again.

A man stood up from a seat that was two rows ahead of us. He asked for Uncle's phone so he could call his family. He said he was an Army major. Just then, we heard a voice from the back of the hall, 'I'm a colonel, but I see that you have a better view of the man so go ahead.'

All this while, Uncle was lying in a recovery position administered by one of the doctors who had taken charge, a smart looking man in his late forties or early fifties. Slowly but surely, he was recovering and the shaking stopped. The doctor helped him to sit up.

'Mister, you're absolutely fine. Don't worry—you just experienced a seizure,' said the doctor. He smoothly replaced Uncle's spectacles on his face and added, 'Do you have any history of epilepsy?'

Uncle didn't say anything. He just adjusted his specs and slowly looked at me. I could hear his eyes say: *You almost killed me today.* In my defence, since I was the closest, I'd like to think that what I did might have helped the man or, at least, brought enough attention to the situation so that people who *could* have helped, finally did.

The crowd murmured. The theatre management escorted the man out of Row 4 and presumably to a taxi to drop him home, and after a few minutes, the play resumed. As for me, all I could think about was the mannerisms of the doctors in the room during this whole thing. Yes, they fought, and some of them were pretty immature, but the way they moved and looked at the old uncle, they instilled confidence. I thought about how I would find a mirror when I got home and to try to capture some of those expressions for future roles. After all, though in real life I may have nearly killed a person with my total ignorance of medical skills and manhandling his body in a completely wrong way, with a little luck, maybe I could still play one on TV.

∿

Avinash Verma is an actor in Mumbai.

Love, 40

Anuradha Sridhar

2013 was one of only two years in the previous ten, in which Roger Federer did not win a grand slam tournament. It was also the year when Martina Hingis reappeared in my life.

If things were right with the world, it ought to have felt like the good old days, except that it wasn't—and they didn't. In March, my husband told me that he's moving out of the apartment that we were provided by his company, and I didn't exactly jump for joy at that. I was left homeless and had to move in with my younger sister Archana until I could find an alternative.

The move was sudden, like the transfers that my father went through when he was working with the Department of

Customs and Excise. The first transfer that I can remember clearly from when I was little, is the one when we moved from Delhi to Chennai. I gave up kathak classes which I really liked, for lessons in Carnatic music which I didn't. By then, I had already developed an interest in tennis. Playing tennis properly is expensive. So there was that, and the fact that I was short of time thanks to the singing; so, I couldn't really play the sport. I continued to watch many matches, quietly read about them and take, at least, some pride in my ability to manage the instability caused by bouncing from one city to another, from one house to another.

A decade later—if one month can be considered one set of tennis—I moved from a long-time single woman to a married woman in two sets. As hurried as the wedding was, it was still an exception in my unhurried life. I had a partner to last my lifetime, and lots of wins to plan for.

The problem was that my partner never really showed up to play. And when he did, he went over to the other side of the court to play against me. I am not a quitter and I don't take timeouts, so the game proceeded at its ugly, sickening pace. From marriage to separation, it plugged along, with plenty of breaks of serve. It went the full five sets, as great tennis matches often do, but it was one of those matches where the outcome was never really in doubt.

At Archana's house, my years of sound sleep gave way to a whole new routine. I spent many, many nights where crying was the last thing I did before falling asleep. And when I woke up a few hours later, crying used to be the very first 'sensation' I experienced. I was upset with myself for shedding tears so often in front of my sister. I was protective of her, right from when we were children, and now the roles had reversed. I lost five kilograms between March and April. I have never dieted in my life, and here I was, following what I called the 'divorce diet' to a T.

Even though I could never narrate the full story—I don't wish to share details that were originally meant for the ears of my husband—I had to narrate it in bits and pieces to several people. It started off with the lawyers. Please forgive the stereotype, but I really had a tough time finding a sane one who wasn't aggressive. A chance phone call with my batchmate from B-school opened up a new path for me. He immediately helped me with a contact. Archana came with me when I went to meet Helen for the first time and I found myself staring at a senior citizen instead of the glamorous young Erin Brockovich look-alike I had pictured in my head. But Helen suited me perfectly. She didn't want to fight for the sake of it; she was reasonable in every sense, and she taught me that advocates and lawyers are not the same thing.

Once that was sorted, the world of friends, acquaintances, colleagues and relatives had to be dealt with. I am referring to these categories very loosely. For me, many colleagues are friends and many relatives are acquaintances, and there are many other combinations. Given the sheer number of people I know, the chatter left me tired. I sought solace in my private blog: A space I had created for myself a couple of weeks before the wedding. It was meant to help me deal with a huge argument that had taken place. I visited the blog over five hundred times—five hundred nights of winter, if you will. Getting it all out is a hugely important process for anyone who's been through a divorce or any traumatic event. You have to recap things, review things that you don't want to think about and you have to see how bad things really are or were, in order to move forward. Some prefer to talk through all of this. I needed to do this in writing.

While all of this was happening with me, Federer was really struggling in the second half of the season. By this, I mean he was ranked #7 in the world—seven! This is incomprehensible to any Federer fan. I mean, I had dealt with second or even third for a few months but *seventh*? No—not for the past ten years. His back trouble coincided with my own aggravated back pain. His misery on Centre Court at Wimbledon, when he lost in the second round, coincided with my misery on the centre court of my life.

Then, Martina Hingis separated from her husband the same year. Hingis and I go back a long way. I came back from school in 1997 to watch her semi-final Wimbledon match against Anna Kournikova. Hingis went on to win that match and then the Wimbledon title a few days later. She was only one year older than me and was playing tennis as a professional. She was winning grand slams, and I was working through class notes on relative velocity and mathematical induction. We really had nothing in common. But now, here she was, going through what I was going through. It's like both she and Federer had decided to remind the world that they were mortals after all, that they had problems and setbacks, conflicts and injuries—the kind you can see as well as the kind you can't see. Just like me.

Right through my marriage, I was feeling like a watered down, constrained, inauthentic version of myself—a version that I couldn't recognize. Since I don't believe in going back in time, the option of going back to what you could call my *original* self, was not available. I didn't know what I was going to become and the loss of my personality left me scared. In my state, I waited out the separation period and flatly refused to succumb to the pressure to file in my birthday month of all months. I signed the paperwork for divorce in December 2013.

It was via mutual consent. One day before we were to submit the forms, his advocate sent an email to me, the only email I have preserved from the marriage. Here's one line worth noting: 'Both parties have agreed to not communicate with each other through texts, blogs, phone calls, emails or any other route for any matter whatsoever in the present or in the future.'

It was: Game. Set. Match.

If you have seen Federer win Wimbledon or the French Open, you would have sometimes seen him crumple to the ground in a mixture of exhaustion and happiness—and, perhaps, disbelief—after the win. In the court I was in—the courtroom rather—the floor was tile and not grass or clay. If it were different, I might have myself crumpled in a strange kind of delight and relief that the endless back and forth was finally over. My victory wasn't over *him*—there are no winners in something like this—but my victory was for me. Maybe I have learned that negotiation and compromise have different shades, some of them truly lovely. Maybe I have learned that the worst of our fears must come true for us to truly acknowledge the courage inside of us. Maybe I have joined a club or something, a select group of people who have been through something intense together, a group that knows what it's like to be Love, 40 down, fight all the way back to deuce, and then on from there.

Anuradha Sridhar is an IIM graduate working at Ernst & Young in Mumbai.

Glaciers Are a Headache

Adi Narayan

A few months ago, I was tagging along with my girlfriend, who's also a journalist like me, and we were in Delhi interviewing a scientist who studies glaciers. And it was quite interesting.

Do you know how many glaciers there are in India? About 10,000. Any guesses on how many of these we're studying, as in, monitoring and so forth?

About ten. That's it. And we ought to be freaked out by that because these glaciers feed all the rivers in north India. Some six hundred million people rely on water from them. And we have literally no idea how climate change is going to affect that.

One reason why no one is studying them is because they are so cold and remote that it makes them very tough places to actually do any research. And there's this scientist, one of India's top glacier experts, who's trying to change that.

His solution is to run a sort of boot camp on the glacier. I found that interesting—not only because 'glacier boot camp' sounds awesome, but also because this professor himself was from Tamil Nadu, where there's just three kinds of weather: hot, very hot and '*What the hell*?' hot. And now he's one of the top experts in the country. And he's recruiting young scientists and sending them up a mountain so they can freeze their butts off—all for the sake of science. There's something about his internal contradictions that I like.

I'm from Tamil Nadu as well, and figured that if he can do it, so can I. So I decided to join their boot camp as a journalist to write about their work. His deputy called me a few days later to screen me and make sure I was legitimate. He asked me who I was, and what I did and so forth; and then he said, 'So what's your climbing experience?'

I said I had climbed mountains here and there, you know, in the Western Ghats, like Matheran, and a mountain in Malaysia.

'Malaysia? What altitude was that?'

'Umm, maybe about 4,500 or 5,000 metres,' I said. 'It felt like that anyway.'

'There is no mountain in South East Asia that high,' he said. 'But this is the bottom line: Are you fit enough to climb with us?'

'For sure! I run every week. And I've even done a marathon.'

I was pretty much the last guy to finish and had to be hospitalized after that, but that detail didn't seem important.

He hesitated. 'Okay, let's do it.'

And so we worked out the dates and I got all the essential goods: hiking boots, sleeping bag, trekking water bottle, indestructible torch, and so forth—because you've got to look like a serious trekker in front of all these people.

I reached Manali and spent a day acclimatizing. And we set off early the next morning towards Rohtang Pass. I think it marks the boundary of the north-western edge of the Vodafone network. I called my girlfriend as we were driving up the mountain road and I said, 'Hey, guess what? I'm on the way to the glacier and there won't be any phone calls after this.'

'Yeah. That's great. I'm washing dishes now, so let me call you back.'

This was the last conversation I had. And I did wonder, that if I were to die on this glacier, the last conversation I had had with a loved one was about how I was less important than cleaning wine glasses.

The road from Manali to Rohtang is good and clear, mostly because there are a zillion tourists who go there every day. And then you cross a ridge and the road just vanishes. It goes from asphalt to rocks, basically. So, bad news if you have any back trouble or are a heart patient.

The scenery was surreal: mountains all around, snowy peaks in the distance and a river gushing down the valley.

Eventually we were at the starting point for the glacier. You walk down to the river and then you cross it by sitting in a basket which is pulled by porters on the other side. Then you climb some more and you're at the basecamp—so, fairly easy. It was at 3,800 metres, or about 12,000 feet—and it was cold. As any of you who've been to the Himalayas would know, when it's sunny, it can be pleasant, but when the sun goes behind a cloud, it gets a special kind of cold.

I met the entire group of students and instructors there, and joined them as they went on a rock-identifying excursion. That's the one thing you find in all geology field trips: They're always pointing at rocks and showing off. You'll be walking along the path, and one of them goes, 'I think that's a mica and silica in that compacted metamorphic rock, man.'

To which, another replies, 'Nahi yaar, that's granite with feldspar.' And the professor waits for a few seconds and then announces that it's tourmaline. And then everybody goes, 'Wow! That's fancy.'

All through my life I've been pretty fit and never really had any seasickness or motion sickness or airsickness or whatever. So I just assumed that this altitude sickness is the same kind of thing; you know, a problem that happens to *other* people.

So on that first day, when my stomach went berserk, I thought it must be a bit of indigestion. It felt as though there were mini bombs going off in there, every half-hour. And then a headache started. The throbbing was minor but then it grew and grew, and eventually, like someone slowly turning up the volume on a radio, got unbearable. I took Crocin, and then Tylenol and whatever else, but nothing worked. Somehow, I fell asleep that first night.

When you think about a glacier, the image you probably get is this vast expanse of sky blue ice, or this long valley of snow. Right? Like those images from Greenland or Antarctica that you've seen on Discovery Channel.

But the thing about Himalayan glaciers is that, for the most part, they're covered with rocks. Scientists tend to call these rocks, 'debris', which lessens the glamour a bit. But these rocks are huge. Each of them is the size of a refrigerator or a washing machine. And they are *everywhere*. You basically have to skip and hop from one to the other to get across. It's fine for about ten or fifteen minutes, but after that, you're just incredibly annoyed.

Within half an hour of starting the trek the next morning,

the pounding headache started again. And I didn't know what to do. I thought it was maybe because of the bright sun, so I put on sunglasses. Or maybe it was the cold, but I was already wearing everything I had—and I was even sweating a little bit.

We reached the spout at about 1 in the afternoon, and you know you're at the spout, because you see a layer of ice and a stream emerging from under it. The glacier begins here, basically.

We had been climbing for about four hours, when Maanya, one of the girls in our group from Bengaluru, suddenly just stopped. We were all walking in a line through these really big boulders and she just froze for about ten seconds. Then she said, 'I can't see anything.'

Her vision became blurred, sort of like when you wear thick glasses. She ignored it at first, but then it happened again. And that totally freaked her out, because nobody had any idea what was causing it. No one was talking so I tried to explain that there is less oxygen at this altitude, and so the body sometimes cuts blood supply to organs for a short time so that the brain can get enough blood. But that explanation freaked her out even more. Sometimes, it's better not to know.

We moved on tentatively when she could see at least a little, and by this time we could see a speck of yellow high up the slope, and that was a huge morale booster. There was a tent, and the site of our camp for the night.

It was a huge relief to get to the camp and get some rest. My plan on the mountain was to interview people while they were climbing and doing experiments and so forth. But I could get nothing done. The headache was so bad at times that I'd just sit inside the tent—my notepad lying inertly at my side—and hope that the pain would magically go away.

About an hour later, there was a lot of commotion at the

camp. When I stepped out of my tent, I found everyone had gathered outside the girls' tent. It turned out that Maanya's blackouts had become more frequent. Her tent-mates were panicking and nothing anyone was trying, was working.

Thupstan, the group leader, eventually decided that Maanya had to go back down—it was just too risky. There was no doctor, and a rumour spread that she might have a condition affected by the altitude, where the brain swells up with fluid. People who get that can die in less than two days. So even though it was 5.30 p.m. and nearly dark, he took her down to the basecamp. That was the last we heard from Maanya up on the mountain, but it was a warning to everyone about the unseen forces acting on all of us every moment of the time that we were up there.

That night after dinner, I was in my tent. I told my tent-mate Virender how my headaches were really bad and that my medicines weren't working. He first offered me Boroline cream and then suggested I take a Dispirin, but I had already done that. Unlike the previous nights, my body couldn't fight through the pain. It was still an unstoppable force when it hit an immovable object—my need for sleep. The pain delivered me crazy dreams, where we were all in some Himalayan village, and the village panchayat was having a meeting about how they need to prevent me from sleeping. Three teams are formed to attack me in the night.

I woke up and noticed that I was sleeping on my side, and when I shifted position to lie on my back, I found that I couldn't move two fingers of my left hand. I was shaking my fingers wildly and my little finger somehow touched my left eye, coming in contact with the eyeball. My finger was numb and so I couldn't feel it; I was still not fully sure if I was awake; all I knew was that my left eye was hurting a lot.

And the first thing that came to mind was that outside the tent were those stupid villagers trying to stop me.

Like a half-asleep, flailing zombie, I decided in a flash, that my two fingers needed to be amputated because of frostbite, and since I had slept with my contact lenses on, they had cut my retina. As all this was happening, I was waving furiously in the tent, and throughout this commotion, Virender was sleeping peacefully, having no idea that I was losing it. It's like I could feel sanity leaving my head. My body was breaking down, but then somehow I lied down again and managed to fall asleep, miraculously. I gathered a sense of reality in the morning and the trek continued.

The next morning we packed up and took part in some scientific activities. This exercise was called the mass-balance measurement and basically involved drilling a deep hole in the ice and putting bamboo rods down, about twenty or thirty metres. Then you come back every year to check how much of the rod is above the ice. You measure the distance and then you know where the ice has melted. You have to do this in some fifty or sixty spots on the glacier, so you have an idea of how fast the whole thing is melting.

After we had finished digging and everyone had taken all their selfies, we started marching to the high camp at 4,900 metres. At this point, every step hurt and my headache seemed to keep getting worse the higher we went. We were walking through an ice and rock zone, and there were crevasses all over the place. A crevasse is a huge crack in the ice—and sometimes the opening can be a metre wide. To get across it, you have to find spots where a rock is stuck on the top. It can be pretty scary and the only thing that gives you the confidence to walk over a big one is seeing the person in front of you not die.

I was pretty much the last guy in the group, and all that time, my mind was creating images of beaches where I could have been. I said to myself: *Next time I'm doing a story on coastal ecosystems. No more mountains.* Meanwhile, the porters were literally running up the rock with twenty or thirty kilos on their backs. One of them even brought an entire LPG gas cylinder all the way to the highest camp so they could cook dal and roti.

We followed slowly.

We were now at the high camp and this was a magical place. The glacier extended out on three sides; you could really see its true size now. And there was a vast expanse of milky white snow extending up the mountains. None of those super annoying boulders were here. In the night, it glowed in the moonlight. Even my headache paused for a second to take in the majesty of the view.

The plan on the last day was to put on special boots and trek to the top of the glacier so we could get some samples. It looked easy, but walking on snow is a really slow process. Unlike the rest of the glacier, this entire zone was covered in a blanket of white, and that meant crevasses and moulins—shafts on glaciers—were hidden everywhere. There were six of us. Thupstan pointed to a distant ridge and said that that's where we were going.

We reached that ridge in about two hours. All this climbing was getting on my nerves and I was eager to finish this up and head back down. But as folks who've climbed snowy peaks would know, there are ridges hidden within ridges. You cross one, and five more appear.

Thupstan says, 'Just one more ridge, guys. You can do it.' And in a slightly lower voice: 'After that, there may be two or three more, I don't know. You can do that, too.'

So we had no choice but to keep walking. At one point along

the way, the guy at the front stepped on a crevasse and went down up to his hip. Thankfully, the girth of his bag blocked the fall. We all tried to pretend that didn't happen.

After the fourth ridge, I was literally at the edge of my strength. The sheer thought of going back down was scary, and my head was throbbing. I could see a giant cloud of mist descending on the mountain from the right. And so I decided to stop right there and promptly fell asleep on the snow. This was at 5,100 metres. The rest of the group went ahead a little and collected chunks of ice for analysis.

Samples in hand, we worked with Thupstan to set up the camp where we would spend our final night.

They had told everyone beforehand to only bring items that we thought were absolutely essential—this was supposed to be a boot camp after all. Some people had brought stuff like chocolates, a Swiss Army knife, Old Monk rum and, of course, Boroline. I brought my Bluetooth speakers. And that meant that when we had the campfire on during the final night, I was the DJ. By popular demand, we blasted 'Baby Doll' and Himesh Reshammiya numbers on that silent glacier. I have a feeling that may have worsened the whole ice melting situation, but that's just my theory.

The next morning was our last morning on this side of the mountain. Just a few hours later, we would be on our way home. My head seemed to sense the end on the horizon because the evil force loosened its grip. Being able to fully focus for the first time in days, I looked out to where we had been and thought about what we had seen. I hadn't known it before, but I learned that the Himalayan glaciers are the third biggest storehouse of frozen water on the planet. The way to understand a glacier's role is to think of them as giant shock absorbers. In cold years, when there's a lot of snowfall, they store more ice. And in the hot years when it rains less, they melt more and there's more water in the rivers. And this natural balance is critical.

Try to imagine for a second what would happen if this balance stopped. Places close to the mountains, like Himachal Pradesh or Uttarakhand, would see massive floods. Tens of millions of people could starve as rivers dry up entirely, in especially hot stretches. The whole of the Sunderbans could disappear. In 2013, in Kedarnath, we had incredible floods. That happened partly because the walls of a glacier lake had burst. Those kinds of catastrophes could happen more often—much more often.

When I think about glaciers now, it's not the snow or the intimidating rocks or even the insane headache that I remember. It's all those people who were so passionate about understanding our mountains. Getting nature to give up her secrets is a really tough job. I'm grateful that there are people doing it, despite the dangers. It takes a special kind of humility I think. Mountains leave you no choice but to be humble, because they remind you of how small you are. They turn you into a listener even if you're not a particularly good one every day. And that was the case with me. I went there to talk, to interview, to write and to capture the experience. But the truth is that it can't be captured. You can never get an actual grip on a glacier.

It's a slippery slope.

Adi Narayan is a journalist and coder in New York.

Tea and Me

Anurag Byas

Tea—better known as chai in India—is a simple milk-based preparation that runs deep through the veins of India. Almost everyone has it in the morning and evening—it's literally everywhere. No proper Bollywood bazaar scene is complete without a tea stall in the background. Tea is to India what beer is to Germany. Like a giant game of 'Six Degrees of Darjeeling', tea has in some way linked everyone on the subcontinent—and I'm no exception. Tea connects people—it's not just Nokia.

Recently, I was in Kerala and a cousin took us sight-seeing. He was keen to impress us, and he drove us from Kollam to Kottayam and then on to Vaghamon, a tea-estate town. We drove through the not-so-straight highways and from one mountain to another. We approached the plantations and I could see a hill on the horizon. As we drove closer to it, I saw the evenly laid out rows of tea plants. They looked immaculate, as if drawn on a canvas. All possible shades of green were spread on rolling hills, like a carpet. I got out of the car, the hum of the engine stopped, and I just soaked in the fragrance of the tea garden. All I could think of was a play on the energy theory: 'Beauty can neither be created nor destroyed; it can just be changed from one form to another'. From this breathtaking scene in Kerala to the refreshing cup on a Mumbai street—the beauty of chai was unwavering.

Like many Indians, tea has been a part of my life's journey through its ups and downs. Many people who know me and who know how much I love tea, would never believe that I didn't try it until I was sixteen. Having my first chai wasn't the rite of passage that it could have been, but something I was forced into.

Back then I didn't drink tea. In my adolescent days, I had a firm belief that God grants your wishes if you give up stuff: The great Renunciation Theory, if you will. As any teenager, I had oodles and oodles of things that I wanted—a video game console, a multi-geared bicycle, free use of the family scooter and good marks in Maths. I told myself that somehow all of this was possible if I gave up tea. In fact, the more society appreciated something, the more valuable it would be for me to give up. Sacrifice small things, get small things. But sacrifice *great* things…

And then as I started to achieve things, it became a self-fulfilling prophecy. So, somehow, tea had gotten caught up in this grand scheme taking place in my head and before I even really knew what was happening, I had preemptively given up tea even before having tried it. Can one really 'give something up' when they've not even had it? Anyway…

Here's how my first cup happened.

I was with my Dad delivering invitation cards in Jodhpur for my brother's wedding. Now, anyone who's delivered wedding cards the old-fashioned way—hand-delivery as opposed to e-invites—knows that there's no way you can walk in, say 'Hi', deliver the card and walk out. Of course, here in India, everyone offers tea—every single house. We were on a mission to deliver about two dozen invites that day. While each visit should have been a small four-step process, it just wasn't. We were spending at least twenty minutes in each house. While my Dad must have had some ten cups of tea, I had avoided as many. With each cup of tea that I managed to stay clear of, my Dad was getting more and more annoyed. After all, the more a host insists and the more you still resist, the ruder you are.

At the end of each visit, he would deliver the card with a smile, wave goodbye, then give me 'the look'. Of course, he didn't know about my devotion to the tea-celibacy vow. To minimize his wrath, I was timing my avoidance strategies much better with each card. At the mere mention of tea in a conversation, I was ready. I would jump right out and say, 'Please don't make it for me.' Some of the hosts did ask me the reason, but I would just shrug my shoulders and smile, a gesture clearly and effectively conveying 'no reason but don't force me, please'. Somehow, it worked.

We were finally at the end of our day and Dad had planned to deliver the last card to his childhood best friend, Mr Trivedi. His house was right in the centre of Jodhpur, just by the foothills of the fort in the centre of the pale blue checkerboard of a city. The sun had set, casting a light purple glow over everything and our host decided to take us up to the terrace for a view. It was an awesome sight. I was so busy exploring the corners of the terrace where monkeys were jumping from roof to roof, that I completely forgot to preemptively refuse my tea. And of course, ten minutes later, three cups of steaming tea followed, with biscuits and namkeen. In other words, the works.

Uncle called me over. I suddenly realized that I had missed my precious window of avoidance and as I walked towards them, my mind started frantically cataloguing plausible excuses that I needed immediately. My hands are, um … my throat feels, um … my face is … but this tea was *made*. It's infinitely more easy to avoid tea which hasn't been made. And before I could utter a word to present my case, Uncle proudly, firmly and with a smile, handed me my first cup of tea. I looked at my Dad, desperately hoping that he would somehow bail me out. Instead, he said, with a certain satisfaction, 'It's getting cold; have it.' And this was how I had my first cup of tea. I have no recollection of how it tasted or whether I liked it. I was defeated, and I wasn't going to give the tea the added satisfaction of being enjoyed.

So this is how we met each other. And we haven't looked back since.

Tea and tea stalls are deep-seated in the fabric of this country. Right from small villages to the busiest of metros, they can be found everywhere. They even stand resilient in the face of the up-market coffee shops that have sprung up throughout the major cities. While these swanky joints with pop music playing in the background cater to only a small slice of the population who can afford ₹200 or more for a coffee, the humble tea stall is for everyone. And, here in India, something as simple and economical as cutting chai is definitely going to outlive the cappuccino. At least, I hope it does. Case in point: There was a high-end coffee outlet in South Mumbai, in front of Café Mondegar, that recently closed but the chaiwallah across the street is going steady and strong. Long live this city!

I love taking the train in Mumbai for both short trips and longer journeys. The Rajasthan Express sells tea almost throughout its sixteen-hour journey. Over the years, the taste has been incredibly consistent, but peculiar things have happened to the quantities. Tea used to be sold in really small shot-glass-sized plastic cups, filled to the brim, for ₹5. Visually, it was satisfying for the customers that they were getting a full glass of tea for a relatively small sum. I noticed after a few years that the tiny plastic glasses made their way to 150 ml styrofoam containers. However, the quantity and price of tea remained the same. Now, visually, people were buying, for the same price, only 'half' a glass of tea. You could hear some people making a fuss over the quantity but the vendors were unrelenting. A few trips later, I realized that the price had doubled. It was ₹10 a cup, but now it was a cupful. By doing so, the price onboard the train was correspondingly moved to ₹10. People were very happy to get a full glass of tea and didn't mind paying even double. Over time, that became the new standard.

But here's the catch. On a recent trip, I noticed that they were now using the original small-sized glasses. But because the glass was full, the price was ₹10. I don't know whether the tea sellers had a convention or what, but there's some serious psychology at work here with glasses, filling them up and then downsizing the containers. It's kind of like the oddly named 'Fun Pack' of Snickers that are really tiny. I don't quite see the 'fun' part. These are magic tricks being played on us and culinary IQ tests we're being subjected to, every day. People who care about tea can't help but notice these things.

In Mumbai, there's a different tea drinking experience around every corner—the guy at the crossing of 33rd and 14th in Khar, who won't let anyone else, including those working for him, make his tea; at Anna's at Mogul Lane in Matunga, you're absolutely expected to play with the dog, Rocket, while sipping; then there's Tea Centre at Churchgate, selling some fifty odd varieties of leaves; and the nondescript stall owner at Cooperage who puts in so much lemongrass and sugar that it tastes pretty much like milky sugar cane juice, but hot.

I found one of the strangest tea sellers in Andheri in the north-west suburbs of our fair city. Mumbaikars might be familiar with the Hindustan Unilever Limited office there. This man has a small room for a shop just across the street. Some years back, when a colleague asked me to accompany him for a round of tea, me being me, I of course couldn't refuse. We just chit-chatted and it took us five minutes to down a cutting chai. Then we started bickering about who would pay and I won (or lost depending on how you look at it). I asked the owner how much and I pulled out two ₹10 notes as I spoke. He said, 'Thirty-four.' I jumped a little and said, 'We just had two cuttings.' He said it was seventeen for one. He just took my curiosity to a whole new level. When I asked him how he was managing to charge three times the usual amount, he told me that he used the best ingredients—he used undiluted milk, only a very particular kind of black pepper, cardamom, and the ginger was absolutely fresh. 'Above all,' he said, 'people pay.' I waited to see how he made his tea. His technique was basic, and just like Po in the movie *Kung Fu Panda*, I learned that there was no secret ingredient. But he had displayed the price clearly and there was even a cautionary statement below the price. And believe me, there were people waiting outside his shop for their turn. The bottom line is that you sure can command a price if you package it well and serve your product with confidence. I'm sure the HUL office across the street had some influence on his marketing skills. Anything in a 'new pack' that comes with a 'new' price would sell. This was a 'unique' tea and I had it for a couple of days. First, I had it by chance; then I had it again to watch how he made it; and the third time was just to be able to brag that I had had a ₹17 cup of tea at least thrice.

And here I am bragging about how I drank three cups of tea for the price of ten.

I'll end with this: I met my wife over a plastic glass of tea. Well, not literally 'met' but we got closer over our walks up to the tea stall on Nariman Point. As is customary in many Mumbai offices, people go out for a short walk after lunch or in the evening, and so did we. We would signal over our shoulder or email that it was time to go and would synchronize our walks to the lift. We would go up to the shop—a short distance away— and ask for two teas. The place was run entirely by women and I felt a motherly touch in their preparations. While their poha and sabudana khichdi were delectable, they never put too much effort into the tea. It was watery and sweet, with a woody aftertaste—a mix of extreme tang and coarseness. I never liked the tea there. But then again, I never went there for good tea. I went there for the good company. And while we eventually stopped having tea there, I held on to the company.

I've been drinking chai now for almost fourteen years. I think I have had fourteen-years-times-four-cups-a-day. I did the math, and that comes out to just about 15,300 cups. And since I didn't get started until I was sixteen, most of you are probably way ahead of me.

Anurag Byas is an investment banker living in Mumbai.

The Proper Channels

Soumitra Singh

The paper trails of Indian government institutions are legendary. Getting a driver's license, procuring a passport, filling out chalaans, or trying to file returns for taxes; each comes with its own custom-designed, mind-numbing labyrinth of officialdom that renders an astonishing elusiveness to even the most simple of tasks.

Even venturing to get an application signed—an ostensibly easy errand—launches you onto a long and arduous journey, where you find yourself manoeuvring through convoluted tiers of hierarchy with archetypical baabus who control their respective universes. To reach your aim, you must please each and every one of these baabus (people that do little more than shuffle papers and bounce you between themselves by displaying their authority through stamps, seals and insignia).

I experienced many minor flirtations with these forces, but only fully encountered their power three times.

Here's the first.

Having studied in various government institutions, I've been exposed to these 'journeys' from an early age. I remember I once tried to apply for a couple of days' leave from my junior college. I was told I had to get a leave application approved from the vice principal of the university. So I wrote a polite letter specifying my days and headed to the vice principal's office. As I attempted to knock on his door, the guard who sat outside the office scowled at me.

'What do you want?' he asked in Marathi filtered with tobacco.

'I want a leave application signed by the vice principal,' I said in Hindi.

The guard pulled a face and rolled his eyes. 'Come tomorrow morning,' he said.

But the following morning I couldn't even get as close to the office as the day before. 'Come later, sahib is busy,' he told me as soon as I rounded the corner.

'What time should I come?'

'Later,' he muttered with clenched teeth.

Keep in mind that all this had occurred before I had learned that the guard was the master of his universe, that is, the master of the universe of getting into the vice principal's office. The guard was the absolute ruler and his supremacy trounced the highest powers-that-be. If there was a God, even God would not be able to enter the vice principal's chamber without the guard's approval. My friends explained this to me when I complained about making a handful of trips without being let into the office.

'You're a complete doofus,' they said. 'Speak to the guard politely, talk in Marathi only, ask about his family and feign interest. Take a box of sweets along—that can help. After all that, then ask to be let into the vice principal's office.'

I thought about this and then I retyped my letter and printed it out, peppering it with a few Marathi words I had learned. But there was no way I was taking a box of chocolates along. With a new attitude, I ventured back into the office the next day.

'Vice principal *kutheaahe?*' I asked the guard as politely as I could in Marathi.

This launched the guard into a string of Marathi, all of which I, of course, couldn't comprehend. While I was nodding along and trying to laugh at all the right parts, I got the sinking feeling I would not be let in again. While reconsidering my previous position on the box of sweets and wondering where I could quickly arrange one from, a door squeaked open and I was ushered into the office mid-conversation with a smile. The vice principal looked up at me and asked what I wanted. On explaining to him that I wanted a leave of two days, he looked at me gravely and asked why I hadn't gotten a letter from my HoD.

'A what?'

'You have to get a letter from your head of department, written on official college stationery, stating that it is acceptable for you to be absent for your desired dates. Get it stamped by the department registrar and then come to me. These things have to go through the *proper channels.*'

And that was the beginning of my journey—a journey to get a leave application signed. A journey that flung me into the dark world of 'applicant table tennis', a world in which I was the ping-pong ball and several tiers of title-wielding baabus and their guards were the paddle holders, bouncing me with Olympic-calibre vigour from one side to the other, complete with spinning, smashing and sweating. Some of these procedures came as tricky hurdles while others came as dead ends. But this is the nature of a system that was designed to establish a set of individuals who are responsible for, but not accountable for, anything.

My second encounter was a few years after junior college.

After four years of engineering at a government university, I was fed up with the red tape my institute had put up. Finally free from its confines, I was glad to be heading out of the place that had led to so much of my bureaucratic frustration. But my dream of a completely hurdle-free freedom was thwarted when I lost my actual engineering degree.

Have you ever lost a degree earned from a government institute? Let me tell you—it's the single most awful thing that could happen to you in the graduation process. That white page which certifies you as an engineer or a doctor or what-have-you—if you have it, treasure it. Do not lose it. Guard it with your life. Put it in a safe with a baby monitor so you can listen to it breathe. When I lost mine, I learned that I had to: A) get an affidavit signed and notarized on special ₹100 stamp paper stating that I'd lost my degree; B) file an FIR at a police station stating that I'd lost my degree and provide a copy of that report to the university; C) take out an advertisement in a daily newspaper stating that I'd lost my degree; and D) meander the halls of my alma mater for months, roaming among gazillions of departments that themselves did not know why they existed. It took me a month of excruciating effort to get from steps A to C, and then the waiting period started for step D.

On one particular Monday, the guard said that the registrar

was out of town and I should come on Friday. On Friday, I was told the dean was out of station and he needed to approve the procedure, and was asked to come next week. The following week, I was told to get the procedure signed by the dean of student affairs and then refer to my HoD before applying for a new degree. When I pleaded to the office clerk, I was told to go to the dean, who ranted and raved at me to come back later or on *any* other day besides today. She was the baabu here, and this was her universe, one in which she was omnipotent and I was a nobody. I once voiced that it had been nearly two months since I'd reapplied but had not gotten the degree yet. I guess that was the absolute wrong thing to say.

'Don't you understand?' she hollered. 'These things need to go through their *proper channels.*'

Proper channels. Where had I heard that phrase before?

It was a phone call with the abusive dean, which my mother overheard, that finally set things into motion. In the words of Mom, 'Something had to be done.' My mother chose the route of relatives, as many people in India do when they need a special task to be completed. She found out that my father's younger brother's wife's second-cousin had a friend who was a friend of the police commissioner of Jaipur. She called him and appealed to his greater sense of humanity (she essentially begged him to recover my obscure engineering degree). I have no idea what he did but within two hours of my conversation with him, the dean called me in person, politely informed me that my degree was ready and asked where she had to come to give it to me. She was going to *deliver* the degree herself. Apparently the threat of someone even more omnipotent entering her universe—kind of like a wormhole I guess—spurned her two-month-old rusting pen into action.

I promptly received my degree the next day, just before joining a new job where said degree needed to be verified. And yes, I could verify it now.

All in all, it was a situation I never want to find myself in again, and I repeat, if you have a degree earned from an Indian government institution, then please guard it with your life. Actually, it's probably more important than your life, because I'm sure *you* will never be as irreplaceable as your government institute degree.

The annoyance of these incidents pales in comparison to my third go around on this ride, which happened at the time I was pursuing my post-graduation studies in Kolkata. As an MBA student, I had decided to pursue a semester abroad as an exchange student in Milan, Italy. I was aware that I was hedged between a government university on the one hand and visa authorities on the other, both of which are infamous for paperwork and the vicissitudes of officialdom. Aware of what I might be entering into, I decided to do a trial-run of sorts—a mini-test in which I filled out my visa application forms, took them to the Italian consulate in Kolkata and asked them to check the documents before I *fully* came and submitted them two weeks later. I headed to the consulate and was greeted by a young sardar ji in a turquoise-blue turban who checked my documents.

'Please print the application on both the front and back pages,' he said sternly. I nodded. 'Please put in the exact dates,' he said when I tried to explain my flight to Italy was not booked yet. 'Where are you paying the fees in Italy?' he asked me.

'It's an exchange program,' I said. 'We don't pay the fees there. I'll be paying fees at my university while the exchange student from Italy will be paying the fees at his own institute.

That's the process of the exchange program.'

He looked at me as if I had three heads. 'Well then, just get an official letter from your university in India saying that you will be paying the fees there.'

Great, I thought to myself. *Another document needed.*

'And you'll probably forget all the things I told you,' he said. 'So I'm going to write them on the back of your application.' In a spidery scrawl, he then penciled his various grievances against my application form on the paper's flip side. I thanked him and promised him I would return two weeks later.

On heading back to my institute, I tried to obtain a letter stating that I would be paying the trimester fees there. 'Why do you need this letter?' the baabu in the administrative department of my university enquired.

'The consulate said I need this letter.'

'Well then… if you need such a letter from us…' the baabu said, cracking his knuckles, 'then get an official letter from the embassy or consulate saying they want such a letter from us.'

I stared, dumbfounded. A letter to say you need a letter. We've entered new existential territory here.

'Wait, but why?'

Again, not the right thing to say.

'You students think you're so clever but you have no idea about the way things are done!' he hollered at my contempt. 'You need an official letter from the university. These things have to go through the *proper channels.*'

And there it was again—a hat-trick.

I won't bore you with the details of obtaining the letter, but I will just mention that I had to go back to the consulate and get a letter, and then get a separate letter from our institute to prove that we were students studying at the university to get the letter saying that we were paying fees at the university; all so that we could just *apply* for the visa. And after two weeks of running around for a few last-minute missing forms, we headed back to the consulate to finally *actually* apply for the visa. The same young sardar ji greeted me—only this time he was wearing a cobalt-blue turban. He remembered me and said 'hello'.

'I see you've still not printed your application front and back,' he said sternly. I felt my world collapse. How could I have forgotten? My nerves were so shot and I was so fragile at this point that he probably could have blown me over.

But before I could fall at his feet and grovel to be forgiven, he interjected, 'It's okay, we'll manage with this,' he said. And then he turned to the next page and said nonchalantly. 'Oh, your passport was issued in Mumbai. You have to apply at the consulate in Mumbai.'

What was he saying? I couldn't have heard him right. He couldn't have just said what he just said.

'You have to apply in Mumbai for a visa since your passport is from Mumbai. You cannot apply here,' he repeated after I'd been staring at him in dumb silence.

'But, but…' My voice remained stuck in my throat. 'I have exams next week and I can't possibly fly to Mumbai at such short notice,' I stammered.

'Listen, you cannot apply here. There's a *proper channel* for these things,' he said.

Of course, there is.

'Well, then why didn't you tell me this when you checked my application two weeks ago?'

He looked at me, thought for a few seconds and then told me the most bald-faced lie I've ever had anyone tell me to my face. He looked me squarely in the eyes and said, 'I have never checked your application.'

That was when I lost it. The anguish I'd felt in all those years of dealing with *proper channels* and worthless protocol spewed forth like molten lava. I started screaming and yelling and pulled out the last page. 'You checked my application, just admit it. This is your idiotic handwriting right here.' I stood up and started recounting how he even recognized me and my form and commented on the page order and then screamed a few phrases that cannot be uttered here but which summarized what he needed to do with this excruciating application, his sadistic job and his miserable life (I don't know where that 'miserable life' came in from, but I did indeed say it—I had some momentum going, after all.) Startled at the commotion, other consulate staff members came over and asked what the matter was. But I was possessed, and was out for blood. I would not let *proper channels* ruin my life anymore.

My outburst seemed to work—or at least do *something*.

A consulate staff member who looked like he could be at a supervisor level, first reprimanded the visa-checking sardar ji and claimed he was new and did not know the actual *proper channels*. (Did the term 'proper channels' just get used in *my* favour?) She then asked me to get proof of residence from my university stating that I did indeed live in Kolkata for my studies. We finally filed the application the next day and received the passport a week later with the Italian visa ensconced within its pages. I had achieved victory against the odds and against another face of the impossible system.

So there you have it. My three tales of dealing with Indian red tape and paper shuffling. My trials of frustration, pain, toil, sorrow and a few laughs. We wait for things to change—and they do, slowly yet steadily—but until then, all we have, to deal with these situations, is our patience, a little bit of humour and, most importantly, the cathartic effect of recounting these traumas to anyone who is willing to listen.

ᔑ

Soumitra Singh is a writer and a strategist who currently works for a hedge fund in New York.

Rescue

Sunny Pawar

Seven years ago, I was like any other man in his early twenties. I had a decent sales job and I had a promising future. I was enjoying my independence. And for the first time in my life, I was earning something. And then I met Aarti, my girlfriend, while working on a promotional campaign for the *Mumbai Mirror* in 2005. I had both, a good job and an amazing girlfriend. In typical Mumbai lingo, '*Mere paas naukri bhi thi aur chokri bhi.*'

With Aarti, life was amazing.

Aarti… how can I describe her? She had a rare combination of childlike innocence and a calming, nurturing aura. She was a cheerful, independent girl, full of fun, love, hope, passion, compassion and much more. Some of Aarti's favourite activities were playing handball, spreading polio awareness and making rangolis.

Aarti always believed in living life to the fullest and that made her special. She saw opportunities in challenges which I never saw. In fact, I saw challenges in opportunities. Aarti's ambition was to become an interior designer, an air hostess, or a social worker. Every day, she had a new career ambition. Her list of goals to be achieved was more exhaustive than even a political party's manifesto.

She was fascinated by Zodiac signs and often tried matching personalities of people with their sun sign traits. Aarti was a true Capricorn as symbolized by the determined yet stubborn goat. I, too—through Aarti—was made to realize the traits of a Scorpio in me. Aarti made me fully aware of those traits with a few blunt examples of my narcissistic behaviour pattern. 'A genuine Scorpio uses sarcasm and exaggeration as the key tools for entertainment,' she said more than once.

Aarti dreamed of having a loving married life. '"A fool in love" makes no sense to me. I only think you are a fool if you don't love,' was her favourite quote. She always believed whatever happens, happens for good.

She enjoyed chatting with me for hours on the Saave Nagar bus stop in Dahisar from where she was supposed to take the bus to her house immediately after reaching the stop. But, every day, we ended up spending several hours there at the stop itself. We then had to pool our next day's snack money for her rickshaw fare so that she could reach home on time.

On a September day almost nine years ago, Aarti called me and told me that she had plans to go out with her college friends. She told me that she wasn't too enthusiastic about going but she didn't want to disappoint the people who had invited her. We spoke to each other around 10 in the morning. A few hours later, she and her friends were riding near Gorai Beach when, for reasons I fully don't know, their car overturned. Most of the people involved, incredibly, had only minor injuries, but Aarti was the worst hit. She suffered from a brain hemorrhage and slipped into coma. Her brain was damaged, not just due to the extent of the injury but also due to the delay in getting her admitted to the hospital immediately. She was put on life support. Every second was extremely precious for her.

Her hair was shaved off completely and vents were put into her head. Aarti's injuries required several operations. She was in the Neuro-Intensive Care Unit (NICU) of Jaslok Hospital for the next four months. I still remember the first night at the hospital clearly. It was agonizingly painful and shattering to the core. They say that, in moments of extreme stress, we tend to go into survival mode—maybe that's what I did as well.

During the next four months, I did what I felt was the right thing to do: Aarti's mom and I took care of Aarti like a newborn child. She was on a ventilator for just under two months—fifty-six days to be exact. It was only around this time that a simple and obvious fact—one that I had been mentally blocking up until then—had started to sink in for me: Life would never be the same for us again.

During the first four months, the sword of death hung over Aarti's head. It was torturous. In the middle of the night the ward boy used to bang—thud, thud, thud—on the door of the annex where the patients' relatives were sleeping and our collective heartbeat would literally stop for a moment because 90 per cent of the time, it meant either someone was dead or about to die.

We were extremely pressed for finances, as the expenses were beyond any middle class family's capacity. Her per-day charge at the NICU was equivalent to my entire month's salary. One day, when I was sitting outside the room and was lost in thought about how to raise money for Aarti's treatment, I came across a news article in *Midday* that mentioned how one economically disadvantaged girl had received financial help for her treatment from newspaper readers. I immediately wrote an email to *Midday* appealing for people to help Aarti. After running from pillar to post, I was finally lucky enough to meet Anand Hola, a reporter who understood the gravity of the situation. She wanted to write about Aarti and, best of all, she wanted to focus on seeing her as a person rather than as a sensational, dramatic news item.

The first feature caused a stir and my constant presence at her bedside made headlines in even bigger newspapers, and before we knew it, our story was covered by a few television channels too. The core of the story was that I had stayed at the hospital for more than hundred days without going home.

According to one paper, Aarti and I became symbols of ultimate love in a cynical city that usually has no time for love. Readers' aid poured in, and we were able to foot her pending bills. Aarti was then shifted to the general ward after four months, though our struggle for finances continued. On the day they moved her, I returned home and slept on my bed for the first time in eighteen weeks. My parents were both happy and shocked. They were happy to see me home, but shocked to see my condition.

From the next day onwards, I left my home every morning and would return by midnight. I would spend the day nursing Aarti. I gave her a bath, changed her clothes and fed her milk. I was completely involved in her care and when I had a chance to take a breather, I had to call people and meet them to arrange for funds for her treatment. This was my routine.

In December 2007, Aarti made progress to the point where her main doctor came to me and told me that she was ready to be cared for at home. However, we still had a long way to go. Aarti was still bedridden and unable to talk, sit, or walk. She could just vaguely acknowledge her mother and my presence as her caregivers but couldn't fully identify us. Sometimes her mother felt that Aarti *did* recognize us but I preferred to quietly deny it in order to have control over my own emotions, to protect my sanity. The right half of her body was completely paralysed. She showed some physical improvements such as an improved appetite and a slight weight gain but, unfortunately, no measurable mental improvements that we could see up to that point. The big positive for us was that we could feed her liquids and semi-solids through her mouth and not through a tube attached to her stomach like we used to do in the hospital. Two people, Aarti's mom and I, who were strangers to each other prior to the accident, gradually became each other's support system.

During this chaotic period, I initially had to quit my CFA course, but I gradually resumed my education after three years. This time I chose to enrol for a Masters in Social Work from Nirmala Niketan College of Home Science. During my fifteen-month stay in Jaslok, I had witnessed the pain and suffering of many people: a mother losing her child, a child losing his mother, a woman losing her husband, friends and relatives dying not just due to illness but due to a shortage of funds. I was lucky enough to raise money for Aarti but there were many who could not save their loved ones no matter how hard they tried. Hence, my sole goal was to learn how to link donors directly with the needy and so I decided to study the development sector.

On 14 June 2010, Aarti had a high fever; she hadn't been well for the past few days. It was raining heavily so we couldn't take her to the doctor. The next day, we took her to the clinic and the doctor said that it seemed serious. She looked pale, afraid and exhausted. He thought she had developed pneumonia. At 8.30 that evening, Aarti breathed her last. We lost our 'four-year-old' child.

I remember how I couldn't comprehend it when the doctor said that she was gone. I looked at him and very normally asked what we should do now. By that I meant to say, 'I see that it's bad but how will we bring her back to life?'

And he bluntly replied, 'Purchase some agarbattis to put near her body until all the relatives arrive.'

Bringing her body back home from the morgue was a gut-wrenching experience for me. I felt as if my soul was bleeding. At this point, I could have easily succumbed to depression. I had a flood of nightmares during those times. Like any person affected by trauma, I went down an extremely dark and scary road. I had become a zombie. We often think of grief as an emotional process, but I also went through physical problems, including eating and sleeping disorders, fatigue and lowered immunity, and other ailments. I remember waking up sometimes in the middle of night and feeling overwhelmed, drained, suffocated—or all of those things at once. Sometimes, I felt like I was cut wide open and sometimes, like I was trapped in my body.

Looking back on those days, I know that I *had* to go through that.

Trauma and grief teach us a lot if we're willing to listen. Pain is inevitable but suffering is optional, they say. Resilience is better than resistance. So I let myself go through it. I waited and didn't punish myself but I also refused to allow myself to sink beyond recovery.

About half a decade later, this process of reorienting myself is still going on. I think it will always be going on. The difference is that now I'm able to see something else; something that I couldn't see for many years: An actual future.

Now, I am trying my best to keep Aarti alive through my work. She was a person who always tried to help people. No matter how difficult our own lives are, we can always add purpose to it by making someone else's life more meaningful. Being kind to others gives us a chance to be kind to ourselves and I initiated my new journey with that mantra.

Currently, I am working for an NGO called Minim Charitable Foundation that works to empower people in the best possible way. Its founding trustee is the legendary Waheeda Rehman ji, one of the most gracious and caring human beings I have ever met in my life. She has not only helped me during my personal struggles but has also provided me this opportunity to achieve my goal of serving people. She has been a motherly mentor to me.

Today, I see tremendous disparity in our society on many different levels—some reflecting ancient ways of thinking and some reflecting unfortunate brand new ones. However, I feel that if drugs, crime and corruption can cut across caste, class and religion, then why can't love, kindness and compassion? And for *that*, we need to unlearn. My dream is to start an academy where people come to unlearn the tendencies they've been reinforcing their whole lives; tendencies that have created far more misery than we deserve as a species.

Today, Aarti would be proud to see her laidback Sunny

trailblazing in his own way. She has, in the truest sense of the word, 'rescued' me.

I am just trying to live up to our shared dream.

∼

Sunny Pawar is a social worker in Mumbai.

Down the Rabbit Hole

Gauri Balani

'When are you getting married?' is a question that can be asked in sixty-seven different ways.

I know.

I have counted.

I have categorized. I have analysed and divided them into nine basic emotional styles.

The Alarmed: 'My God! At this rate, you're never going to be married, are you?'

The Angry: 'If you're so picky, how do you expect to get married?'

The Bribing: 'Don't you wish for your own house and husband to manage?'

The Concerned: 'Sweetheart, isn't it time you were married?'

The Curious: 'How come you're not married yet? Something wrong with you?'

The Demanding: 'So, when are you inviting us for *your* wedding dinner?'

The Pitying: 'Oh, you poor thing. When will *you* go shopping for a diamond necklace with your fiancé?'

The Romantic: 'You will find the *one* someday, right?'

…And, the Zany: 'It's okay to come out of the closet. We won't judge.'

I have been fielding these questions for well over fifteen years now. When it started being asked, like any well-developed skill, my parents coached me by example: jokes, abrupt answers, blank stares, more jokes and a standard answer of 'Not yet' were my training wheels.

Insidiously though, soon enough, the question started being asked by my parents themselves. 'So, beta, should we put an ad in the newspaper for you?'… or 'This community matrimonial service has contacted us. Should we respond?'… quickly turning into, 'Be home by six. We have to go meet the boy' and 'For god's sake, if not for your own self, learn to put on some makeup and behave like a girl!'

I must admit that last one hurt. After so many years of being told that I am like a son, and can do everything (in the process of becoming a doctor) from dissecting a human body at age seventeen to giving sex advice to fifty-year-olds at age twenty-one, that statement was a bit harsh. I don't think I even knew what they meant by 'behave like a girl'.

After all the advertisements in the newspaper and recommendations by aunties, my parents still weren't able to marry me off. I actually cooperated the best I could and gave into their more 'reasonable' demands, such as fasting only on water for three days and going to a temple, six hours' drive away—all in the name of accumulating good karma and getting a husband like Lord Shiva.

As time went by, the matrimonial conversation waxed and waned in our house, eventually dulling to a background murmur. In the meantime, I managed to go to Yale for my Master's; live and travel by myself; and establish a career I could be proud of. Then, when I hit a certain milestone—I won't define which one—I thought to myself: *It is time I got married*. Having only ever experienced the route of marriage agencies and newspaper ads to find a husband, I did the 'now' version of it—I put up my profile on a matrimonial website.

And with that, I stepped into a surreal world.

I completely understood what Alice must have felt like falling down that rabbit hole. Either I was too big (a polite version of too fat), or I was too small (polite version of too short). I was too educated, or not rich enough. 'Oh, you're in *India*. I thought you had a green card' or 'Oh you're in *India*. You never told me you didn't have a green card'. Never was there a door that I could walk through just the way I was. I went from bemused to plain amused pretty quickly. Yet I did not take my profile off, still optimistic that maybe there was a soul out there like me, who didn't know any other channel for finding a person he wanted to marry.

One day, I got a call at 8.00 p.m.; a polite hour—not too early and not too late. It was from an unlisted number. Now, in India, unlisted numbers are pretty rare. I debated whether to pick it up at all, but then decided to pick it up, thinking to myself: *What the heck! I've never gotten a call from an unlisted number before*. (It's amazing how sometimes life takes a complete turn due to such small incidents.) A rich, deep voice politely wished me a good evening and promptly introduced himself. He gave a reference of the matrimonial site and asked if it was a good time to talk. That, in itself, was such a pleasant change from the usual calls from the site that I found myself encouraging conversation. We talked for an exact ten minutes and ended it pleasantly with the pledge to talk some more the day after. Lo and behold, the next night I got a call exactly at the time he had promised, and this time the call lasted much longer.

Our conversations got a little deeper with each subsequent call and a little more detailed about our lives. He was a space engineer, working for NASA and loaned out to DARPA in Boston, Massachusetts. He had a four-bedroom waterfront condo at a complex in Cambridge (which I, of course, googled immediately while on the phone). He had been too busy with his education and career to find someone he wanted to marry. He had put his profile on the matrimonial site because he was optimistic that maybe there was a soul out there like him, who didn't know any other channel for finding a person they wanted to marry. He had a well-stocked library and Shakespeare and Sherlock Holmes were his favourite reads. He complimented me on the witty slogan on a t-shirt I was wearing in a photograph, before complimenting me on my pretty eyes. Honestly, it was wonderful. It was like talking to someone who had been custom-made to my preferences.

Of course, he had a past. Doesn't everyone of a certain age? He said he had dated a Pakistani girl in his university, who was now a well-known politician, famous for her good looks and her Birkin handbags. Things didn't work out because her family insisted on him moving to Pakistan, something that's not a small deal in India. The cynical side of me whispered a very soft 'far-fetched story' at this point, which I obviously ignored, thinking: *Maybe it is possible, is it not?*

After about a month, he announced that he would be coming to India for a six-month project to work with the space program here; some sort of a joint training program with the US government.

We would finally get to meet.

I went into a pleasant tizzy, planning my travel to Mumbai where he would be based, overlooking the fact that the Indian space program is usually conducted out of Chennai. He said he'd let me know when he would have some time off after coming to India, as he wanted to spend time with me without distractions of work, which I thought was a great idea. So I booked an open ticket and gave a heads up at work that I might take a few days off, final dates pending. Two and half months of stimulating conversations made for a genuine anticipation of the meeting. I won't say I had rose-coloured glasses on yet, but they were definitely in my hand, ready and waiting.

Soon after, the phone calls stopped abruptly.

I was a little puzzled; then concerned; then annoyed. After two weeks, I got a call from him again; this time, from an Indian number.

So he *was* in India!

He apologized profusely and was so sorry to have slipped off the radar as he was travelling on a federal plane and the security restrictions prevented him from letting me know when he was flying. He had pleaded with them to let him call from the plane and although he couldn't, I loved that he tried.

He was in Mumbai and he very much wanted to meet me, but he could not predict when he would get time off.

'Could we please talk on the phone in the meantime?' He

pleaded so gently and was so very contrite, that I agreed. And this time, I had his phone number too, so I could call anytime and talk if I really wanted to.

Another fortnight went by. On the phone, he wittily described his quirky Indian project-mates and his daily struggle with the local lack of basic technology needed for a cutting-edge space program. He told me about how he kept flying off to Delhi to meet his politician uncle, who's now retired. He also described his ancestral house in Lucknow, which his other uncle had laid informal claim to, but which actually belonged to him. He decried the resultant family feud that he did not want to be a part of.

After another week, we talked about his work, more about me, and things we had in common. At one point he told me that he was getting a fantastic deal for a piece of prime real estate, courtesy of the defence personnel quota. It was to be developed as a gated community, very close to the projected new airport just outside of Mumbai. He almost whispered about what a dream it would be to have somewhere to be close to our parents. It was practically at a throwaway price, so maybe there was something wrong with it, but he had double-checked with some sources and couldn't find a reason against it at the moment. He had already made arrangements for two parcels of land. Only, due to his citizen status, he had a limitation of how much he could invest. The shortfall was ₹15 lakh (or about $23,000).

Would I like to invest that amount? The title deed for one of them was to be in my name, of course. My cynical alter ego popped its head up. It was a moot point anyway, I told myself. I didn't have that kind of money to invest and so, I honestly told him that. He was definitely disappointed, but quickly apologized for even thinking of asking me to consider mobilizing that kind of money. After all, he was the man and it was his duty, he said, to take care of me and my family. He would ask his uncle to invest. I was not to worry my head; one of the title deeds would still be in my name. Still, it would have been nice if I had shown some 'commitment' to building a trusting relationship with him.

I again reiterated the fact that it was nothing to do with trust; I genuinely did not have that kind of money to invest. He was again incredibly contrite for asking me something like this since we hadn't even met yet, and I, of course, did not really know him *that* well. His apologies were very charming.

A week later, my office planned a very opportune meeting for me in Mumbai, just before a long weekend. So, I called him up and we arranged to meet at ITC Grand Maratha for dinner, Friday night. A little background about the Grand Maratha: It's a gorgeous, five-star heritage hotel boasting of award-winning, Michelin star restaurants and where the room rents run into thousands of US dollars.

He had been booked into a suite for the six months that he was to be in India.

On that Friday, I walked into the lobby at 8.00 p.m. as we had planned, went up to the receptionist and confidently asked her to call up to the room to let him know that I was waiting. She very naturally asked me the room number. I did not have it. I just mentioned his name and assumed that since he was a guest for so long, she would know. She replied that it was against hotel policy to confirm the names of guests staying at the hotel and she was so sorry but she couldn't help me if I didn't know the room number. After a five-minute futile conversation with the receptionist and the supervisor, I gave up and tried his cell phone. The response alternated from endless rings to 'this phone is switched off'. At this point, I was equal parts concerned and annoyed. After about ten minutes, he finally picked up the phone. Again, abject apologies ensued—he was actually returning from a meeting and was stuck in traffic (ubiquitous in Mumbai) and in a bad signal zone. He asked me if I could please hang around the lobby and promised he would be there as soon as he possibly could. Of course, I'd wait.

Forty-five minutes later, an almost unrecognizable version of his photograph walked into the lobby. For a minute, I was not even sure if it was the same guy. He walked up to me with me a huge smile and uttered a deep-voiced 'hello'. At least his voice was the same. A few minutes of apologizing later, he asked me to wait and walked up the reception. After a brief, flirtatious conversation with the receptionist, he came back with a key and invited me up to his room. Forget the cynical alter ego; my logical side was giving off flashing red lights and sounding alarm bells. I politely declined and said I would wait for him in the lobby. He grew more and more insistent and I grew even a little rude, I confess. Finally, after laying a guilt trip on me for not trusting him even after meeting him, he took me to the exclusive lobby meant for only the guests staying in the suites. He spoke to the bartender like a long-lost friend and told him to take care of me and walked into the suite just opposite.

As an aside, I must confess I felt a little foolish for being so doubting. I berated my cynical alter ego for being so strident. It would still not shut up and I had this heated debate all by myself in my head, just like in *Alice in Wonderland*.

Finally, I started the conversation with him, over a lavish, elaborate dinner, by talking about movies and whether he liked Hollywood or Bollywood movies; turned out, neither. I casually mentioned my favourite rom-com being *How to Lose a Guy in*

10 Days, but it drew a blank from him. He started talking about the car ride he had just shared with a colleague, discussing the investment project we had talked about before. He mentioned again how great it was and perhaps we could go see the land the next day if I wanted to. He talked about how, for a measly ₹15 lakh, I would get assets worth millions in my name for me to do whatever I wanted to.

I let him wax eloquent for a little while; took a big breath; and then I started talking. I talked about how I wished to get married right away, how I always wanted a big family and my entire extended family close by and how I couldn't wait for a brood of kids kicking the ball around in the big front yard—plus the fact that biological imperative demanded that I have kids right away. In fact, I babbled about how I always dreamt of being a homemaker and was ready to give up my career as soon as I got married and how I would love for my mother to live with me; and my sister's family, too—one big happy family (without a mother-in-law, of course).

His response? His top secret space mission had him on medications that made him impotent—and sterile—with no chance of recovery. And for ₹15 lakh, I could buy my mum a wonderful big house just outside of Mumbai in a secure, gated community—full of retired military big shots, no less. In fact, if I wished, for 10 more lakh, he would get a third piece of land for my sister, too!

I stared at him, took a long sip of wine, and then gushed over him for being so considerate of my family and told him I would love to go see the project the very next day. In fact, I would invite my lawyer uncle and my brother along, too. He had to meet my family eventually after all; why not now? I reassured him it didn't matter to me that he was sterile; we could always adopt like Angelina Jolie: One kid from every country we travelled to.

Now I could see sweat building up on his forehead. I asked him very sweetly whether he was alright and why was he turning so pale. He tried to look relaxed. 'I thought you lived with your mum already and didn't really have a big family. You never mentioned a lawyer uncle and a brother who works in the CBI and the fact that I would have to meet them.' I replied that I was very close to my family and cherished their opinions about major life-changing decisions like marriage. I said we should decide on a time to meet the next day to go see the project he was so enthusiastic about. Moreover, if possible, why not go to Delhi and Lucknow with my uncle and see if we could get his ancestral property back?

It was very natural for him to get a work call just then, which precluded further conversation.

And of course, the phone was switched off the next day.

And it was no surprise to me to read an article in the *Hindustan Times* a week later about a man arrested for defrauding a widow of ₹25 lakh by promising her marriage and then asking her to invest in a great project for a gated community just outside of Mumbai.

I don't know why, but I kept my profile up, even after all of this. Maybe it was because I didn't want this one encounter to deter me from the 'needle in a haystack' possibility. Maybe it was just a kind of resignation that to play this game at all means to play it online these days. Not only is it still up there, but I do still check it from time to time; both the hopeful and masochistic sides of me curious about what's lurking behind every click.

And so, just like Alice, I sometimes wander into the surreal world of matrimonial websites once in a while:

To talk of many things:
Of shoes—and ships—and sealing wax—
Of cabbages—and kings—
And why the sea is boiling hot—
And whether pigs have wings.

Gauri Balani is a public health doctor in Mumbai.

Rickrolled

Sridhar Gorthi

It was the summer of 1984 in hot and sweaty Delhi. I was twelve, going on twenty-one, with all the typical angst involved in that messy transition from boy to 'not-boy-but-not-quite-man'.

I was a typical 80s kid—completely unremarkable; short for my age; skinny, with a katori-cut fringe; and perpetually skinned knees. In case you don't know, katori means 'small bowl'. The katori-cut is achieved—if you can call it that—by the head being covered by a katori and then cutting off all the remaining bits you can see. Think, Friar Tuck.

And I was sick of it.

I was desperate to stand out and yearned to be taken seriously.

Let me elaborate a bit. As with most such stories of boyhood angst, the central figure of my personal opera was, of course, a girl. Her name was Anjali and she was vivacious, funny, pretty, and most importantly, just a little bit shorter than me.

A large part of my life was spent daydreaming about ways of winning her attention. They were mostly elaborate fantasies involving improbable rescues from burning buildings; she, in my arms and my hair flowing in the wind like Fabio. I was tired of being too small. Girls would laugh at my jokes but then glance over my shoulder at the older guys to check to see if they had been laughing too. I wanted to be like those guys, with their baggy trousers and fearless hairstyles—mohawks, mullets, elaborate sweeps, and coifs. This was the 80s, remember? I didn't want to be nice—and, most certainly, not sweet. I wanted to be noticed—particularly by Anjali.

And then suddenly, an opportunity presented itself in the rather ample shape of Pummy aunty from the US. This was way before cable TV and Coca-Cola, and back in those days, the only cars you could buy in India were Fiats and Ambassadors (and exactly one model of each). NRIs seemed to be made of money in those days. I went to welcome Pummy aunty and she casually gave me ₹10 since she'd forgotten to get me a gift. 'Buy yourself something you like.' Casual; just like that: Ten whole rupees!

Mum disapproved of the extravagance, but she wasn't going to make me give it back. There was this unwritten code, you see. I had done nothing wrong, so there would be no disapproval of me. The tenner was mine. The disapproval was reserved for Pummy aunty, 'who really should have known better'.

I knew *exactly* what I was going to do with the money. I was going to get a haircut. Not the usual katori cut, of course. This was going to be special. I was going to go to Andre's. Andre's was to me, the Mecca of barber shops—the full wall mirror; the gold (or, at least, bronze) finishings; the fully working, adjustable red leather chairs; and of course, all the mysterious instruments and tonics, all lined up just right. And so I'd made this plan—my date with Andre. This would work. It had to. What better way to impress a woman?

But the haircut would cost ₹15 and I only had ten. Thoughts of how to make up for the rest of the money consumed me. My newspapers were all sold already. And no one wanted my perfectly acceptable Michael Jackson *Thriller* cassette. Just when I was feeling defeated, I glanced up at the poster in my room. It was a racing motorbike, taking a super sharp turn on a track, and above it, read: 'A winner never quits, and a quitter never wins'. I had to press on.

I had no choice but to go to Rana. Poor Rana—wheezy, clingy, desperate-for-my-friendship Rana. I was not proud of what I had to do, but fate left me no choice. Ten more was no problem for him.

'Actually, I only need five,' I told him.

'But what about the tip?'

I didn't even know about it. Imagine my embarrassment. Rana saved me in more ways than one.

I now had ₹20—more than I'd ever had in my life. There was a building expectation of emerging transformed, no longer a boy with the uniform fringe of the masses—but a man. I wanted something artistic but not obscene: A sweep of hair from one side to another, making a lovely curving flow across my forehead; short on the sides with a tapering tail down the back to the nape of my neck. Think, Rick Astley.

The only thing that pushed my hair out of my daydreams was Anjali's possible reaction. I'd finally decided that the situation would play out like this: She'd look at me, perking up with interest over this cool 'new guy', only to realize who it was! She'd be flustered, I decided, blushing prettily, stammering a little as she wondered what to say. I'd be blasé about it, of course; playing it cool, smiling casually. 'Hey Angie,' I'd say… or maybe, 'Ange'? No no. That sounds like a skin condition. I'd reply, 'What? My hair? Oh yeah, I forgot about it.'

Before I knew it, there I was—right in front of Andre's.

Picture this: My money carefully counted and kept safe in my pocket, and my stomach feeling weirdly empty, like I hadn't eaten in days. The fact that I was the shortest kid in the salon did not help with my nerves. The walls of the place were covered with pictures of impossibly handsome guys looking off into the distance with different hairstyles to choose from. But of course, I already knew exactly what I wanted. On closer inspection, Andre's fell just a little short of the imagined ideal. Bits of hair on the floor, leather chairs looking ancient and a bit worse for wear, and an overriding smell of disinfectants.

But, no; push those thoughts aside. These guys were *professionals*. This was going to work. This was Andre's, after all.

And now it was my turn, finally. My stylist was a skinny young man, complete with acne spots and dirty nails, whose frayed name tag read 'Alan'.

Wait, what?

Ah, but then he went to work. He started to flick my hair this way and that, seemingly figuring out what style would suit me best.

Yes, yes! I could feel my body unclench as I settled into the chair with a wiggle, and the leather yielded and moulded to the contours of my bum.

I kept my eyes closed, and then when the snipping slowed

like the very last popcorn kernels popping, I opened them.

This is it!

Ok, maybe not *exactly* what I wanted, but close enough.

Wait—even *better*, actually. The sweep up from the front is there, and there's the shorter crop on the sides. Even the one errant strand that dared to not obey Alan, now artfully flicked perfectly into place.

Would it have been better to have it a bit longer from the back, maybe?

No, no. It's fine. It's more than fine. Alan has earned his tip, fair and square.

I don't even remember cycling back home. It was like I was drifting on air; hot flushes of excitement exploding in my chest. Of course, I would have to deal with Mum when I got to the house, but that was a small price I'd happily pay.

Mum's reaction was difficult to decipher. Was that a tiny hint of a smile right there?

Nah, she's probably just amazed that her little boy could look so grown up.

'Beta, you didn't tell me you were getting a haircut,' she said, her tone non-committal. I shrugged, nonchalant. I'm a cool guy now.

I went to my room and stood in front of my mirror, trying on different looks to compliment my hair. They all worked— jacket and dark glasses; casual pullover; regular t-shirt. My new hair was going to make everything look so damn good—after it settled in a bit, perhaps.

Modelling was suddenly a very real career option, I thought to myself.

Dinner was a rushed affair. I was preoccupied with a million thoughts, playing out all kinds of 'new me' scenarios, mostly involving Anjali. Perhaps for the first time in my life, I wished that I could delete Sunday and fast forward to school on Monday morning.

First thing on Sunday morning, my Mum told me to go take a bath. I had bits of hair sticking to my body, so I didn't argue. Shower done, I headed for the mirror. My damp hair was plastered to my head, but no cause for concern. I watched carefully how Alan had pulled the front out and then back to create the classic raised sweep effect with a roller brush. It should be easy enough to do with a comb, too, although I made a mental note to invest in a roller brush sometime soon.

Hmm…it was now flopping over disconcertingly. But my hair was still damp. I didn't have a blow dryer, but a thorough toweling and five to ten minutes in the sun should do the trick, I reckoned. I stepped out on the verandah vigorously scrubbing my head. *Ah, that was better.*

Carefully engage comb… Gently pull forward and flick back… Flop. Flick. Flick. Flop.

What the hell!

Okay, once more—even more slowly this time…

Damn. No, no, it was the flick I was getting wrong. That part had to be done with a quick wrist action…

Still no luck.

I could hear Mum calling me for breakfast. My face was blank as I tried the special manoeuvre for the tenth time without success. Then, tears began to prick my eyes as I pressed the comb into my scalp painfully, trying desperately to find a way to get it right. It was hopeless. Jagged spikes stuck out on the top of my head and a longer portion flopped stupidly to one side. Utterly hopeless!

Mum was outside the bathroom door. 'Everything okay, beta?'

No, no! It's not okay! Everything is utterly crap and there's nothing anyone can do about it. How the hell am I going to face Anjali like this? And don't even get me started on what the other boys are going to do to me. Couldn't I just spend the rest of my life in the loo? There was water here and I could sleep on the towels. Anything would be better than facing the world, looking like a cross between a porcupine and a freshly-sheared sheep.

But Mum was relentless and starting to get worried.

I finally emerged from the bathroom to an exclamation of surprise by Mum.

'Beta... your hair...'

And I just couldn't hold it in any longer. I burst into tears and clung to my Mum. It was all so unfair! She just held on to me and let me get it out of my system like she usually did. As I subsided into sobs and sniffles, Mum held me at arm's length.

'Here, let me have a look now. Let's see what we can do with this.'

Ultimately, there was really nothing much that could be done. Mum explained that my ambition would require hair products, special brushes and blow-drying, which, obviously, I wasn't going to be able to do every morning (even assuming I had my own tools and accessories). She snipped off some of the most offending bits and finally managed to make things look relatively neat and normal. I was back to being a little boy again: Sadder—maybe a little bit wiser—but still just a boy.

My eyes still felt raw from the crying, and the crushing disappointment of Sunday morning had settled into a dull ache by the time I reached school on Monday. I firmly suppressed all thoughts of the pleasant fantasies I'd built up for this moment— dwelling on those would only bring me to tears again, and if anyone saw me crying in school, it would really be the end of life as I knew it.

'Your hair looks funny.'

I knew that voice.

I turned. 'Thank you, Anjali. Good morning to you, too.'

She laughed. 'Sorry! It's just that it's sticking out a bit from the back.'

I said something clever then, I think; something self-deprecating. I can't remember exactly what. But then, just like that, we got chatting and laughing. And she came and sat next to me during Chemistry class. We became good friends. All was well. I wish I could say that the chemistry continued outside of the classroom, too, but six months later, she changed schools and I never saw her again. Unsurprisingly, life went on.

And so I learned an important life lesson that day: Confidence and a sense of humour will always get you a lot further than a fancy hairstyle. As a bald man now, I still see the wisdom in that, and consider it an extremely useful lesson, regardless of how things turned out on the top of my own head.

∽

Sridhar Gorthi is a lawyer in Mumbai.

This book isn't finished!
What's *your* story? Use the blank pages that follow
to brainstorm.
Live in India? Send your true, personal story to
story@talltales.in for consideration as part of an upcoming
live performance of Tall Tales. The stories we like most are
between 1,000- and 2,000-words long and told from the
first-person perspective.
Don't live in India? Find a storytelling event near you—
or better yet, start one yourself.

www.talltales.in